AUDUBON GUIDE
to the National Wildlife Refuges

Rocky Mountains

D0950462

AUDUBON GUIDE
to the National Wildlife Refuges

Rocky Mountains

Colorado · Idaho · Montana
Utah · Wyoming

By John Grassy

Foreword by Theodore Roosevelt IV

Series Editor, David Emblidge

A Balliett & Fitzgerald Book
St. Martin's Griffin, New York

AUDUBON GUIDE TO THE NATIONAL WILDLIFE REFUGES: ROCKY MOUNTAINS. Copyright © 2000 by Balliett & Fitzgerald, Inc.

All rights reserved. Printed in Hong Kong. No part of this book may be used or reproduced in any manner whatsoever without written permission except in the case of brief quotations embodied in critical articles or reviews. For information, address St. Martin's Press, 175 Fifth Avenue, New York, N.Y. 10010.

National Audubon Society® is a registered trademark of the National Audubon Society, Inc.

Cartography: © Balliett & Fitzgerald, Inc. produced by Mapping Specialists Ltd.
Illustrations: Mary Sundstrom
Cover design: Michael Storrings and Sue Canavan
Interior design: Bill Cooke and Sue Canavan

Balliett & Fitzgerald Inc. Staff
Sue Canavan, Design Director
Maria Fernandez, Production Editor
Alexis Lipsitz, Executive Series Editor
Rachel Deutsch, Associate Photo Editor
Kristen Couse, Associate Editor
Paul Paddock, Carol Petino Assistant Editors
Howard Klein, Editorial Intern

Balliett & Fitzgerald Inc. would like to thank the following people for their assistance in creating this series:
At National Audubon Society:
 Katherine Santone, former Director of Publishing, for sponsoring this project
 Claire Tully, Senior Vice President, Marketing
 Evan Hirsche, Director, National Wildlife Refuges Campaign
At U.S. Fish & Wildlife Service:
 Richard Coleman, former Chief, Division of Refuges, U.S. Fish & Wildlife Service
 Janet Tennyson, Outreach Coordinator
 Craig Rieben, Chief of Broadcasting & Audio Visual, U.S. Fish & Wildlife Service, for photo research assistance
 Pat Carrol, Chief Surveyor, U.S. Fish & Wildlife Service, for map information
 Regional External Affairs officers, at the seven U.S. Fish & Wildlife Service Regional Headquarters
 Elizabeth Jackson, Photographic Information Specialist, National Conservation Training Center, for photo research
At St. Martin's Griffin:
 Greg Cohn, who pulled it all together on his end, as well as Michael Storrings and Kristen Macnamara
At David Emblidge—Book Producer:
 Marcy Ross, Assistant Editor
Thanks also to Theodore Roosevelt IV and John Flicker.

ISBN 0-312-24574-2
First St. Martin's Griffin Edition: March 2000

10 9 8 7 6 5 4 3 2 1

CONTENTS

MONTANA

UTAH

WYOMING

Appendix

Foreword

America is singularly blessed in the amount and quality of land that the federal government holds in trust for its citizens. No other country can begin to match the variety of lands in our national wildlife refuges, parks and forests. From the Arctic Refuge on the North Slope of Alaska to the National Key Deer Refuge in Florida, the diversity of land in the National Wildlife Refuge (NWR) System is staggering.

Yet of all our public lands, the National Wildlife Refuge System is the least well known and does not have an established voting constituency like that of the Parks System. In part this is because of its "wildlife first" mission, which addresses the needs of wildlife species before those of people. That notwithstanding, wildlife refuges also offer remarkable opportunities for people to experience and learn about wildlife—and to have fun doing so!

The Refuge System was launched in 1903 when President Theodore Roosevelt discovered that snowy egrets and other birds were being hunted to the brink of extinction for plumes to decorate ladies' hats. He asked a colleague if there were any laws preventing the president from making a federal bird reservation out of an island in Florida's Indian River. Learning there was not, Roosevelt responded, "Very well, then I so declare it." Thus Pelican Island became the nation's first plot of land to be set aside for the protection of wildlife. Roosevelt went on to create another 50 refuges, and today there are more than 500 refuges encompassing almost 93 million acres, managed by the U.S. Fish & Wildlife Service.

The Refuge System provides critical habitat for literally thousands of mammals, birds, amphibians and reptiles, and countless varieties of plants and flowers. More than 55 refuges have been created specifically to save endangered species. Approximately 20 percent of all threatened and endangered species in the United States rely on these vital places for their survival. As a protector of our country's natural diversity, the System is unparalleled.

Setting NWR boundaries is determined, as often as possible, by the needs of species that depend on the protected lands. Conservation biology, the science that studies ecosystems as a whole, teaches us that wildlife areas must be linked by habitat "corridors" or run the risk of becoming biological islands. The resulting inability of species to transfer their genes over a wide area leaves them vulnerable to disease and natural disasters. For example, the Florida panther that lives in Big Cypress Swamp suffers from a skin fungus, a consequence, scientists believe, of inbreeding. Today's refuge managers are acutely aware of this precarious situation afflicting many species and have made protection of the System's biodiversity an important goal.

Clearly, the job of the refuge manager is not an easy one. Chronic underfunding of the System by the federal government has resulted in refuges operating with less money per employee and per acre than any other federal land-management agency. Recent efforts by some in Congress to address this shortfall have begun to show results, but the System's continued vulnerability to special interests has resulted in attempts to open refuges to oil drilling, road building in refuge wilderness areas, and military exercises.

The managers of the System have played a crucial role in responding to the limited resources available. They have created a network of volunteers who contribute tens of thousands of hours to help offset the lack of direct financing for the Refuge System. Groups like refuge "friends" and Audubon Refuge Keepers have answered the call for local citizen involvement on many refuges across the country.

I hope Americans like yourself who visit our national wildlife refuges will come away convinced of their importance, not only to wildlife but also to people. I further hope you will make your views known to Congress, becoming the voice and voting constituency the Refuge System so desperately needs.

—*Theodore Roosevelt IV*

Preface

Thank you for adding the *Audubon Guide to the National Wildlife Refuge System* to your travel library. I hope you will find this nine-volume series an indispensable guide to finding your way around the refuge system, as well as a valuable educational tool for learning more about the vital role wildlife refuges play in protecting our country's natural heritage.

It was nearly 100 years ago that Frank Chapman, an influential ornithologist, naturalist, publisher and noted Audubon member, approached President Theodore Roosevelt (as recounted by Theodore Roosevelt IV in his foreword), eventually helping to persuade him to set aside more than 50 valuable parcels of land for the protection of wildlife.

Because of limited funding available to support these new wildlife sanctuaries, Audubon stepped up and paid for wardens who diligently looked after them. And so began a century of collaboration between Audubon and the National Wildlife Refuge System. Today, Audubon chapter members can be found across the country assisting refuges with a range of projects, from viewing tower construction to bird banding.

Most recently, National Audubon renewed its commitment to the Refuge System by launching a nationwide campaign to build support for refuges locally and nationally. Audubon's Wildlife Refuge Campaign is promoting the Refuge System through on-the-ground programs such as Audubon Refuge Keepers (ARK), which builds local support groups for refuges, and Earth Stewards, a collaboration with the U.S. Fish and Wildlife Service and the National Fish and Wildlife Foundation, which uses refuges and other important bird habitats as outdoor classrooms. In addition, we are countering legislative threats to refuges in Washington, D.C., while supporting increased federal funding for this, the least funded of all federal land systems.

By teaching more people about the important role refuges play in conserving our nation's diversity of species—be they birds, mammals, amphibians, reptiles, or plants—we have an opportunity to protect for future generations our only federal lands system set aside first and fore-most for wildlife conservation.

As a nation, we are at a critical juncture—do we continue to sacrifice wetlands, forests, deserts, and coastal habitat for short-term profit, or do we accept that the survival of our species is closely linked to the survival of others? The National Wildlife Refuge System is a cornerstone of America's conservation efforts. If we are to leave a lasting legacy and, indeed, ensure our future, then we must build on President Theodore Roosevelt's greatest legacy. I invite you to join us!

—John Flicker, President, National Audubon Society

Introduction
to the National Wildlife Refuge System

He spent entire days on horseback, traversing the landscape of domed and crumbling hills, steep forested coulees, with undulating tables of prairie above. The soft wraparound light of sunset displayed every strange contour of the Badlands and lit the colors in each desiccated layer of rock—yellow, ochre, beige, gold.

Theodore Roosevelt was an easterner. As some well-heeled easterners were wont to do, he traveled west in 1883 to play cowboy, and for the next eight years he returned as often as possible. He bought a cattle ranch, carried a rifle and a six-gun, rode a horse. North Dakota was still Dakota Territory then, but the Plains bison were about gone, down to a scattering of wild herds.

The nation faced a new and uneasy awareness of limits during Roosevelt's North Dakota years. Between 1776 and 1850, the American population had increased from 1.5 million to more than 23 million. National borders were fixed and rail and telegraph lines linked the coasts, but Manifest Destiny had a price. The ongoing plunder of wildlife threatened species such as the brown pelican and the great egret; the near-total extermination of 60 million bison loomed as a lesson many wished to avoid repeating.

Despite the damage done, the powerful landscapes of the New World had shaped the outlooks of many new Americans. From Colonial-era botanist John Bartram to 19th-century artists George Catlin and John James Audubon, naturalists and individuals of conscience explored the question of what constituted a proper human response to nature. Two figures especially, Henry David Thoreau and John Muir, created the language and ideas that would confront enduring Old World notions of nature as an oppositional, malevolent force to be harnessed and exploited. The creation in 1872 of Yellowstone as the world's first national park indicated that some Americans, including a few political leaders, were listening to what Thoreau, Muir, and these others had to say.

Roosevelt, along with his friend George Bird Grinnell, drew upon these and other writings, as well as their own richly varied experiences with nature, to take the unprecedented step of making protection of nature a social and political cause. Of his time in the Badlands, Roosevelt remarked "the romance of my life began here," and "I never would have been president if it had not been for my experiences in North Dakota." As a hunter, angler, and naturalist, Roosevelt grasped the importance of nature for human life. Though he had studied natural history as an undergraduate at Harvard, believing it would be his life's work, Roosevelt owned a passion for reform and had the will—perhaps need—to be effective. Rather than pursuing a career as a naturalist, he went into politics. His friend George

Barren-ground caribou

Arctic Ocean

Alaska

Bering
Sea

Pacific Ocean

Washington

Oregon

Idaho

Montana

North
Dakota

South
Dakota

Wyoming

Nebrask

Nevada

Utah

Colorado

Kansa

California

Oklah

Pacific
Ocean

Arizona

New
Mexico

Texas

Midway

Hawaii

Pacific Ocean

New England Region
Middle Atlantic Region
Southeast Region
Northern Midwest Region
South Central Region
Southwest Region
Rocky Mountains Region
Alaska and Pacific Northwest Region
California and Hawaii Region

Migratory Flyway

Great Lakes

Minnesota

Michigan

Wisconsin

Iowa

Illinois

Indiana

Ohio

Missouri

Kentucky

Tennessee

Arkansas

Mississippi

Alabama

Louisiana

New Hampshire
Vermont
Massachusetts

Maine

New York

Rhode Island
Connecticut

Pennsylvania

New Jersey

Delaware

Maryland

West Virginia

Virginia

North Carolina

South Carolina

Georgia

Florida

Atlantic Ocean

Puerto Rico

Gulf of Mexico

Bird Grinnell, publisher of the widely read magazine *Forest and Stream,* champi-
oned all manner of environmental protection and in 1886 founded the Audubon
Society to combat the slaughter of birds for the millinery trade. Fifteen years later,
TR would find himself with an even greater opportunity. In1901, when he inher-
ited the presidency following the assassination of William McKinley, Roosevelt
declared conservation a matter of federal policy.

Roosevelt backed up his words with an almost dizzying series of conservation
victories. He established in 1903 a federal bird reservation on Pelican Island,
Florida, as a haven for egrets, herons, and other birds sought by plume hunters. In
eight years, Roosevelt authorized 150 million acres in the lower 48 states and
another 85 million in Alaska to be set aside from logging under the Forest Reserve
Act of 1891, compared to a total of 45 million under the three prior presidents. To
these protected lands he added five national parks and 17 national monuments. The
NWR system, though, is arguably TR's greatest legacy. Often using executive order
to circumvent Congress, Roosevelt established 51 wildlife refuges.

The earliest federal wildlife refuges functioned as sanctuaries and little else.
Visitors were rare and recreation was prohibited. Between 1905 and 1912 the first
refuges for big-game species were established—Wichita Mountains in Oklahoma,

Atlantic puffins, Petit Manan NWR, Maine

the National Bison Range in
Montana, and National Elk
Refuge in Jackson, Wyoming.
In 1924, the first refuge to
include native fish was created;
a corridor some 200 miles
long, the Upper Mississippi
National Wildlife and Fish
Refuge spanned the states of
Minnesota, Wisconsin, Illi-
nois, and Iowa.

Still, the 1920s were dark
years for America's wildlife.
The effects of unregulated
hunting, along with poor
enforcement of existing laws,
had decimated once-abundant
species. Extinction was feared
for the wood duck. Wild turkey

had become scarce outside a few southern states. Pronghorn antelope, which today
number perhaps a million across the West, were estimated at 25,000 or fewer. The
trumpeter swan, canvasback duck, even the prolific and adaptable white-tailed
deer, were scarce or extirpated across much of their historic ranges.

The Depression and Dust-bowl years, combined with the leadership of
President Franklin Delano Roosevelt, gave American conservation—and the
refuge system in particular—a hefty forward push. As wetlands vanished and fertile prairie soils blew away, FDR's Civilian Conservation Corps (CCC) dispatched
thousands of unemployed young men to camps that stretched from Georgia to
California. On the sites of many present-day refuges, they built dikes and other

Saguaro cactus and ocotillo along Charlie Bell 4WD trail, Cabeza Prieta NWR, Arizona

water-control structures, planted shelterbelts and grasses. Comprised largely of men from urban areas, the experience of nature was no doubt a powerful rediscovery of place and history for the CCC generation. The value of public lands as a haven for people, along with wildlife, was on the rise.

In 1934, Jay Norwood "Ding" Darling was instrumental in developing the federal "Duck Stamp," a kind of war bond for wetlands; hunters were required to purchase it, and anyone else who wished to support the cause of habitat acquisition could, too. Coupled with the Resettlement Act of 1935, in which the federal government bought out or condemned private land deemed unsuitable for agriculture, several million acres of homesteaded or settled lands reverted to federal ownership to become parks, national grasslands, and wildlife refuges. The Chief of the U.S. Biological Survey's Wildlife Refuge Program, J. Clark Salyer, set out on a cross-country mission to identify prime wetlands. Salyer's work added 600,000 acres to the refuge system, including Red Rock Lakes in Montana, home to a small surviving flock of trumpeter swans.

The environmental ruin of the Dust bowl also set in motion an era of government initiatives to engineer solutions to such natural events as floods, drought, and the watering of crops. Under FDR, huge regional entities such as the Tennessee Valley Authority grew, and the nation's mightiest rivers—the Columbia, Colorado, and later, the Missouri—were harnessed by dams. In the wake of these and other federal works projects, a new concept called "mitigation" appeared: If a proposed dam or highway caused the destruction of a certain number of acres of wetlands or other habitat, some amount of land nearby would be ceded to conservation in return. A good many of today's refuges were the progeny of mitigation. The federal government, like the society it represents, was on its way to becoming complex enough that the objectives of one arm could be at odds with those of another.

Citizen activism, so integral to the rise of the Audubon Society and other groups, was a driving force in the refuge system as well. Residents of rural Georgia applied relentless pressure on legislators to protect the Okefenokee Swamp. Many other refuges—San Francisco Bay, Sanibel Island, Minnesota Valley, New Jersey's Great Swamp—came about through the efforts of people with a vision of conservation close to home.

More than any other federal conservation program, refuge lands became places where a wide variety of management techniques could be tested and refined. Generally, the National Park system followed the "hands off" approach of Muir˙and Thoreau while the U.S. Forest Service and Bureau of Land Management, in theory, emphasized a utilitarian, "sustainable yield" value; in practice, powerful economic interests backed by often ruthless politics left watersheds, forests, and grasslands badly degraded, with far-reaching consequences for fish and wildlife. The refuge system was not immune to private enterprise—between 1939 and 1945, refuge lands were declared fair game for oil drilling, natural-gas exploration, and even for bombing practice by the U.S. Air Force—but the negative impacts have seldom reached the levels of other federal areas.

Visitor use at refuges tripled in the 1950s, rose steadily through the 1960s, and by the 1970s nearly tripled again. The 1962 Refuge Recreation Act established guidelines for recreational use where activities such as hiking, photography, boating, and camping did not interfere with conservation. With visitors came opportunities to educate, and now nature trails and auto tours, in addition to beauty, offered messages about habitats and management techniques. Public awareness of wilderness, "a place where man is only a visitor," in the words of long-time advocate Robert Marshall of the U.S. Forest Service, gained increasing social and political attention. In 1964, Congress passed the Wilderness Act, establishing guidelines for designating a host of federally owned lands as off-limits to motorized vehicles, road building, and resource exploitation. A large number of refuge lands qualified—the sun-blasted desert of Arizona's Havasu refuge, the glorious tannin-stained waters and cypress forests of Georgia's Okefenokee Swamp, and the almost incomprehensible large 8-million-acre Arctic NWR in Alaska, home to vast herds of caribou, wolf packs, and bladelike mountain peaks, the largest contiguous piece of wilderness in the refuge system.

Sachuest Point NWR, Rhode Island

Nonetheless, this was also a time of horrendous air and water degradation, with the nation at its industrial zenith and agriculture cranked up to the level of "agribusiness." A wake-up call arrived in the form of vanishing bald eagles, peregrine falcons, and osprey. The insecticide DDT, developed in 1939 and used in World War II to eradicate disease-spreading insects, had been used throughout the nation ever since, with consequences unforeseen until the 1960s. Sprayed over wetlands, streams, and crop fields, DDT had entered watersheds and from there the food chain itself. It accumulated in the bodies of fish and other aquatic life, and birds consuming fish took DDT into their systems, one effect was a calcium deficiency, resulting in eggs so fragile that female birds crushed them during incubation.

Partially submerged alligator, Anahuac NWR, Texas

Powerful government and industry leaders launched a vicious, all-out attack on the work of a marine scientist named Rachel Carson, whose book *Silent Spring*, published in 1962, warned of the global dangers associated with DDT and other biocides. For this she was labeled "not a real scientist" and "a hysterical woman." With eloquence and courage, though, Carson stood her ground. If wild species atop the food chain could be devastated, human life could be threatened, too. Americans were stunned, and demanded an immediate ban on DDT. Almost overnight, the "web of life" went from chalkboard hypothesis to reality.

Protecting imperiled species became a matter of national policy in 1973 when President Nixon signed into law the Endangered Species Act (ESA), setting guidelines by which the U.S. Fish & Wildlife Service would "list" plant and animal species as *threatened* or *endangered* and would develop a program for their recovery. Some 56 refuges, such as Ash Meadows in Nevada and Florida's Crystal River, home of the manatee, were established specifically for the protection of endangered species. Iowa's tiny Driftless Prairie refuge exists to protect the rare, beautifully colored pleistocene land snail and a wildflower, the northern monkshood. Sometimes unwieldy, forever politicized, the ESA stands as a monumental achievement. Its successes include the American alligator, bald eagle, and gray wolf. The whooping crane would almost surely be extinct today without the twin supports of ESA and the refuge system. The black-footed ferret, among the rarest mammals on earth, is today being reintroduced on a few western refuges. In 1998, nearly one-fourth of all threatened and endangered species populations find sanctuary on refuge lands.

More legislation followed. The passage of the Alaska National Interest Lands Conservation Act in 1980 added more than 50 million acres to the refuge system in Alaska.

The 1980s and '90s have brought no end of conservation challenges, faced by an increasingly diverse association of organizations and strategies. Partnerships now link the refuge system with nonprofit groups, from Ducks Unlimited and The Nature Conservancy to international efforts such as Partners in Flight, a program to monitor the decline of, and to secure habitat for, neotropical songbirds. These cooperative efforts have resulted in habitat acquisition and restoration, research, and many new refuges. Partnerships with private landowners who voluntarily offer marginally useful lands for restoration—with a sponsoring conservation group cost-sharing the project—have revived many thousands of acres of grasslands, wetlands, and riparian corridors.

Coyote on the winter range

Citizen activism is alive and well as we enter the new millennium. Protecting and promoting the growth of the NWR system is a primary campaign of the National Audubon Society, which, by the year 2000, will have grown to a membership of around 550,000. NAS itself also manages about 100 sanctuaries and nature centers across the country, with a range of opportunities for environmental education. The National Wildlife Refuge Association, a volunteer network, keeps members informed of refuge events, environmental issues, and legislative developments and helps to maintain a refuge volunteer workforce. In 1998, a remarkable 20 percent of all labor performed on the nation's refuges was carried out by volunteers, a contribution worth an estimated $14 million.

A national wildlife refuge today has many facets. Nature is ascendant and thriving, often to a shocking degree when compared with adjacent lands. Each site has its own story: a prehistory, a recent past, a present—a story of place, involving people, nature, and stewardship, sometimes displayed in Visitor Center or Headquarters exhibits, always written into the landscape. Invariably a refuge belongs to a community as well, involving area residents who visit, volunteers who log hundreds of hours, and a refuge staff who are knowledgeable and typically friendly, even outgoing, especially if the refuge is far-flung. In this respect most every refuge is a portal to local culture, be it Native American, cows and crops, or big city. There may be no better example of democracy in action than a national wildlife refuge. The worm-dunker fishes while a mountain biker pedals past. In spring, birders scan marshes and grasslands that in the fall will be walked by hunters. Compromise is the guiding principle.

What is the future of the NWR system? In Prairie City, Iowa, the Neal Smith NWR represents a significant departure from the time-honored model. Established in 1991, the site had almost nothing to "preserve." It was old farmland with scattered remnants of tallgrass prairie and degraded oak savanna. What is happening at Neal Smith, in ecological terms, has never been attempted on such a scale: the reconstruction, essentially from scratch, of a self-sustaining 8,000-acre native biome, complete with bison and elk, greater prairie chickens, and a palette of wildflowers and grasses that astonish and delight.

What is happening in human terms is equally profound. Teams of area residents, called "seed seekers," explore cemeteries, roadside ditches, and long-ignored patches of ground. Here and there they find seeds of memory, grasses and wildflowers from the ancient prairie, and harvest them; the seeds are catalogued and planted on the refuge. The expanding prairie at Neal Smith is at once new and very old. It is reshaping thousands of Iowans' sense of place, connecting them to what was, eliciting wonder for what could be. And the lessons here transcend biology. In discovering rare plants, species found only in the immediate area, people discover an identity beyond job titles and net worth. The often grueling labor of cutting brush, pulling nonnative plants, and tilling ground evokes the determined optimism of Theodore and Franklin Roosevelt and of the CCC.

As the nation runs out of wild places worthy of preservation, might large-scale restoration of damaged or abandoned lands become the next era of American conservation? There are ample social and economic justifications. The ecological justifications are endless, for, as the history of conservation and ecology has revealed, nature and humanity cannot go their separate ways. The possibilities, if not endless, remain rich for the years ahead.

—John Grassy

How to use this book

Local conditions and regulations on national wildlife refuges vary considerably. We provide detailed, site-specific information useful for a good refuge visit, and we note the broad consistencies throughout the NWR system (facility set-up and management, what visitors may or may not do, etc.). Contact the refuge before arriving or stop by the Visitor Center when you get there. F&W wildlife refuge managers are ready to provide friendly, savvy advice about species and habitats, plus auto, hiking, biking, or water routes that are open and passable, and public programs (such as guided walks) you may want to join.

AUDUBON GUIDES TO THE NATIONAL WILDLIFE REFUGES

This is one of nine regional volumes in a series covering the entire NWR system. **Visitable refuges**—over 300 of them—constitute about three-fifths of the NWR system. **Nonvisitable refuges** may be small (without visitor facilities), fragile (set up to protect an endangered species or threatened habitat), or new and undeveloped.

Among visitable refuges, some are more important and better developed than others. In creating this series, we have categorized refuges as A, B, or C level, with the A-level refuges getting the most attention. You will easily recognize the difference. C-level refuges, for instance, do not carry a map.

Rankings can be debated; we know that. We considered visitation statistics, accessibility, programming, facilities, and the richness of the refuges' habitats and animal life. Some refuges ranked as C-level now may develop further over time.

Many bigger NWRs have either "satellites" (with their own refuge names) separate "units" within the primary refuge or other, less significant NWRs nearby. All of these, at times, were deemed worthy of a brief mention.

ORGANIZATION OF THE BOOK

■ **REGIONAL OVERVIEW** This regional introduction is intended to give readers the big picture, touching on broad patterns in landscape formation, interconnections among plant communities, and diversity of animals. We situate NWRs in the natural world of the larger bio-region to which they belong, showing why these federally protected properties stand out as wild places worth preserving amid encroaching civilization.

We also note some wildlife management issues that will surely color the debate around campfires and

ABOUT THE U.S. FISH & WILDLIFE SERVICE Under the Department of the Interior, the U.S. Fish & Wildlife Service is the principal federal agency responsible for conserving and protecting wildlife and plants and their habitats for the benefit of the American people. The Service manages the 93-million-acre NWR system, comprised of more than 500 national wildlife refuges, thousands of small wetlands, and other special management areas. It also operates 66 national fish hatcheries, 64 U.S. Fish & Wildlife Management Assistance offices, and 78 ecological services field stations. The agency enforces federal wildlife laws, administers the Endangered Species Act, manages migratory bird populations, restores nationally significant fisheries, conserves and restores wildlife habitats such as wetlands, and helps foreign governments with their conservation efforts. It also oversees the federal-aid program that distributes hundreds of millions of dollars in excise taxes on fishing and hunting equipment to state wildlife agencies.

congressional conference tables in years ahead, while paying recognition to the NWR supporters and managers who helped make the present refuge system a reality.

■ **THE REFUGES** The refuge section of the book is organized alphabetically by state and then, within each state, by refuge name.

There are some clusters, groups, or complexes of neighboring refuges administered by one primary refuge. Some refuge complexes are alphabetized here by the name of their primary refuge, with the other refuges in the group following immediately thereafter.

■ **APPENDIX**

Nonvisitable National Wildlife Refuges: NWR properties that meet the needs of wildlife but are off-limits to all but field biologists.

Federal Recreation Fees: An overview of fees and fee passes.

Volunteer Activities: How you can lend a hand to help your local refuge or get involved in supporting the entire NWR system.

U.S. Fish & Wildlife General Information: The seven regional head-quarters of the U.S. Fish & Wildlife Service through which the National Wildlife Refuge System is administered.

National Audubon Society Wildlife Sanctuaries: A listing of the 24 National Audubon Society wildlife sanctuaries, dispersed across the U.S., which are open to the public.

Bibliography & Resources: Natural-history titles both on the region generally and its NWRs, along with a few books of inspiration about exploring the natural world.

Glossary: A listing of specialized terms (not defined in the text) tailored to this region.

Index

National Audubon Society Mission Statement

PRESENTATION OF INFORMATION: A-LEVEL REFUGE

■ **INTRODUCTION** This section attempts to evoke the essence of the place, The writer sketches the sounds or sights you might experience on the refuge, such as sandhill cranes taking off, en masse, from the marsh, filling the air with the roar of thousands of beating wings. That's a defining event for a particular refuge and a great reason to go out and see it.

■ **MAP** Some refuges are just a few acres; several, like the Alaskan behemoths, are bigger than several eastern states. The scale of the maps in this series can vary. We recommend that you also ask refuges for their detailed local maps.

■ **HISTORY** This outlines how the property came into the NWR system and what its uses were in the past.

■ **GETTING THERE** General location; seasons and hours of operation; fees, if any (see federal recreation fees in Appendix); address, telephone. Smaller or remote refuges may have their headquarters off-site. We identify highways as follows: TX14 = Texas state highway # 14; US 23 = a federal highway; I-85 = Interstate 85.

Note: Many NWRs have their own web pages at the F&W web site, http://www.fws.gov/. Some can be contacted by fax or e-mail, and if we do not provide that information here, you may find it at the F&W web site.

■ **TOURING** The **Visitor Center**, if there is one, is the place to start your tour. Some have wildlife exhibits, videos, and bookstores; others may be only a kiosk. Let someone know your itinerary before heading out on a long trail or into the backcountry, and then go explore.

Most refuges have roads open to the public; many offer a wildlife **auto tour,** with wildlife information signs posted en route or a brochure or audiocassette to guide you. Your car serves as a bird blind if you park and remain quiet. Some refuge roads require 4-wheel-drive or a high-chassis vehicle. Some roads are closed seasonally to protect habitats during nesting seasons or after heavy rain or snow.

Touring also covers **walking and hiking** (see more trail details under ACTIV-ITIES) and **biking.** Many refuge roads are rough; mountain or hybrid bikes are more appropriate than road bikes. When water is navigable, we note what kinds of **boats** may be used and where there are boat launches.

■ **WHAT TO SEE**

Landscape and climate: This section covers geology, topography, and climate: primal forces and raw materials that shaped the habitats that lured species to the refuge. It also includes weather information for visitors.

Plant life: This is a sampling of noteworthy plants on the refuge, usually sorted by habitat, using standard botanical nomenclature. Green plants bordering watery places are in "Riparian Zones"; dwarfed trees, shrubs, and flowers on windswept mountaintops are in the "Alpine Forest"; and so forth.

Wildflowers abound, and you may want to see them in bloom. We give advice about timing your visit, but ask the refuge for more. If botany and habitat relationships are new to you, you can soon learn to read the landscape as a set of interrelated communities. Take a guided nature walk to begin.

(Note: In two volumes, "Plants" is called "Habitats and Plant Communities.")

Animal life: The national map on pages 4 and 5 shows the major North American "flyways." Many NWRs cluster in watery territory underneath the birds' aerial superhighways. There are many birds in this book, worth seeing simply for their beauty. But ponder, too, what birds eat (fish, insects, aquatic plants), or how one species (the mouse) attracts another (the fox), and so on up the food chain, and you'll soon understand the rich interdependence on display in many refuges.

Animals use camouflage and stealth for protection; many are nocturnal. You may want to come out early or late to increase your chances of spotting them. Refuge managers can offer advice on sighting or tracking animals.

Grizzly bears, venomous snakes, alligators, and crocodiles can indeed be dangerous. Newcomers to these animals' habitats should speak with refuge staff about precautions before proceeding.

■ ACTIVITIES Some refuges function not only as wildlife preserves but also as recreation parks. Visit a beach, take a bike ride, and camp overnight, or devote your time to serious wildlife observation.

Camping and swimming: If not permissible on the refuge, there may be federal or state campgrounds nearby; we mention some of them. Planning an NWR camping trip should start with a call to refuge headquarters.

Wildlife observation: This subsection touches on strategies for finding species most people want to see. Crowds do not mix well with certain species; you

---

A NOTE ON HUNTING AND FISHING Opinions on hunting and fishing on federally owned wildlife preserves range from "Let's have none of it" to "We need it as part of the refuge management plan." The F&W Service follows the latter approach, with about 290 hunting programs and 260 fishing programs. If you have strong opinions on this topic, talk with refuge managers to gain some insight into F&W's rationale. You can also write to your representative or your senators in Washington.

For most refuges, we summarize the highlights of the hunting and fishing options. You must first have required state and local licenses for hunting or fishing. Then you must check with refuge headquarters about special restrictions that may apply on the refuge; refuge bag limits, for example, or duration of season may be different from regulations elsewhere in the same state.

Hunting and fishing options change from year to year on many refuges, based on the size of the herd or of the flock of migrating birds. These changes may reflect local weather (a hard winter trims the herd) or disease, or factors in distant habitats where animals summer or winter. We suggest what the options usually are on a given refuge (e.g., some birds, some mammals, fish, but not all etc.). It's the responsibility of those who wish to hunt and fish to confirm current information with refuge headquarters and to abide by current rules.

> **COMMON SENSE, WORTH REPEATING**
>
> **Leave no trace** Every visitor deserves a chance to see the refuge in its pristine state. We all share the responsibility to minimize our impact on the landscape. "Take only pictures and leave only footprints," and even there you'll want to avoid trampling plant life by staying on established trails. Pack out whatever you pack in. Ask refuge managers for guidance on low-impact hiking and camping.
>
> **Respect private property** Many refuges consist of noncontiguous parcels of land, with private properties abutting refuge lands. Respect all Private Property and No Trespassing signs, especially in areas where native peoples live within refuge territory and hunt or fish on their own land.
>
> **Water** Protect the water supply. Don't wash dishes or dispose of human waste within 200 ft. of any water. Treat all water for drinking with iodine tablets, backpacker's water filter, or boiling. Clear water you think is OK may be contaminated upstream by wildlife you cannot see.

may need to go away from established observation platforms to have success. Learn a bit about an animal's habits, where it hunts or sleeps, what time of day it moves about. Adjust your expectations to match the creature's behavior, and your chances of success will improve.

Photography: This section outlines good places or times to see certain species. If you have a zoom lens, use it. Sit still, be quiet, and hide yourself. Don't approach the wildlife; let it approach you. Never feed animals or pick growing plants.

Hikes and walks: Here we list specific outings, with mileages and trailhead locations. Smooth trails and boardwalks, suitable for people with disabilities, are noted. On bigger refuges, there may be many trails. Ask for a local map. If you go bushwacking, first make sure this is permissible. Always carry a map and compass.

Seasonal events: National Wildlife Refuge Week, in October, is widely celebrated, with guided walks, lectures, demonstrations, and activities of special interest to children. Call your local refuge for particulars. At other times of the year there are fishing derbies, festivals celebrating the return of migrating birds, and other events linked to the natural world. Increasingly, refuges post event schedules on their web pages.

Publications: Many NWR brochures are free, such as bird and wildflower checklists. Some refuges have pamphlets and books for sale, describing local habitats and species.

Note: The categories of information above appear in A and B refuges in this book; on C-level refuges, options are fewer, and some of these headings may not appear.

—*David Emblidge*

Rocky Mountains
A Regional Overview

There is no escape out here from the recognition that nature is ascendant. There is simply too much of it, and in near mythic proportions. Views stretch for 10 to 60 miles or more, across valleys like inland seas, walled in by peaks, range upon range of peaks. Some are sharp edged and toothy, others are broad backed. They touch the clouds, summits white with snow, lower areas clad in black-green forests of pine and fir.

Not that anyone is looking to escape. The tremendously varied natural worlds of the Rocky Mountain states—in this guide, Colorado, Idaho, Montana, Utah, and Wyoming—are a source of wonder and renewal for visitors and residents alike.

A splendid sampling of natural diversity is found at the 22 national wildlife refuges of the Rockies region covered here. Visitors can walk along some of the nation's great rivers—the Green, Rio Grande, Snake, and Missouri—in landscapes ranging from cool, forested bottomlands to beautifully desiccated badlands and cliffs of desert rock. In high, well-watered valleys, spring wildflowers color expanses of greening meadows, while streams and rivers, loud with running snowmelt, tumble across the floor. Everywhere there's wildlife: the elegance of shorebirds, swans, and sandhill cranes; the stoic gaze of a bison; the regal, wary elk; the silhouette of a golden eagle drifting through prairie sky.

Trumpeter swan

There are many human stories here as well—of American Indian life, of mountain men and women, of homesteaders, Butch Cassidy and Stuart's Stranglers, and the wartime legacy of the Rocky Mountain Arsenal.

NATIVE PEOPLES

Following the eastern flanks of the Continental Divide from Canada south to New Mexico, the Old North Road for many hundreds of years was a travel route used by American Indians—and the likely route taken by their ancestors, some of

American bison　　　　whom settled in the Southwest perhaps 12,000 years earlier. Traveling the road were

9

Coeur d'Alene

16

11

Great Falls

12

13

M o n t a n a

14

Helena ★

Billings

17

I d a h o

7 ★ Boise

6

Idaho Falls

21

Jackson

Pocatello

8

10

W y o m i n g

5

Great Salt Lake

18

Ogden

22

Green River

Salt Lake City ★

Provo

3

20

19

U t a h

Grand
Junction

St. George

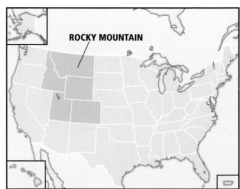

ROCKY MOUNTAIN

15

Casper

Laramie • ★ Cheyenne

4
★ Denver

C o l o r a d o

• Colorado Springs

Pueblo •

1

ROCKY MOUNTAINS

COLORADO
1 Alamosa–Monte Vista
   NWR Complex
2 Arapaho NWR
3 Browns Park NWR
4 Rocky Mountain Arsenal NWR

IDAHO
5 Bear Lake NWR
6 Camas NWR
7 Deer Flat NWR
8 Grays Lake NWR
9 Kootenai NWR
10 Minidoka NWR

MONTANA
11 Benton Lake NWR
12 Bowdoin NWR
13 Charles M. Russell NWR
14 Lee Metcalf NWR
15 Medicine Lake NWR
16 National Bison Range
17 Red Rock Lakes NWR

UTAH
18 Bear River
    Migratory Bird Refuge
19 Fish Springs NWR
20 Ouray NWR

WYOMING
21 National Elk Refuge
22 Seedskadee NWR

Spring wildflowers, Red Rock Lakes NWR, Montana

members of many Plains tribes—the Blackfeet, Shoshone, and Crow, the Cheyenne, Arapaho, and Sioux; to the south, in Colorado and east into the Great Basin were the Ute and Jicarilla. West of the Divide were many others, including the Nez Perce, Salish, and Kootenai, whose yearly harvest of food included Pacific salmon that migrated into many rivers of present-day Idaho.

In the early 1840s, five chiefs of the Blackfeet nation journeyed out to see the world. They traveled the Old North Road from their home on the plains of Alberta down to present-day Taos, New Mexico. Their trip lasted three years. The historian William Brandon observed that these chiefs may well have been the last American Indians to follow this route in peace.

GEOLOGY

Indians of the region called it "the backbone of the world," a description that even today retains essential truths. Winding for 25,000 miles from Alaska to the tip of South America, the Continental Divide—with the Rocky Mountains its most dramatic North American feature—is a shaper of worlds. It splits the region's watersheds into east and west, Atlantic and Pacific; and where the Rockies loom highest, it fosters two climates, one wetter, one drier.

Youthful by the measure of geologic time, today's Rocky Mountains began their ascent about 60 million years ago, as tectonic plates well beneath the earth's

crust began to slide and shift and push upon one another. The pressure of this movement caused great blocks of crust to fracture and over time to move in several ways. Some fell downward to be overtopped by others; some were compressed or folded. Each movement represents a specific type of faulting; different mountain ranges across the region are the products of one or more of these events, which continue today.

Seismic chaos was only the beginning. Ensuing wet and dry periods spanning millions of years moved enormous loads of sediment produced as the mountains wore down. The vast Wyoming Basin, encompassing southwestern Wyoming and northwest Colorado, is a mountain graveyard, with peaks entombed beneath its gentle terrain. Water and wind ate away at the soft sedimentary lands of north-central Montana, sculpting the labyrinth of coulees and badlands known as the Missouri Breaks.

Today beneath Yellowstone National Park is a powerful hotspot, a plume of molten rock. One theory holds that the continent has been creeping westward over this inferno for eons. Idaho's Snake River Plain, inundated by lava flows as recent as 2,000 years ago, was shaped by its passage over the hotspot. Volcanic eruptions have long been a feature of this area, including the massive explosion 600,000 years ago that formed Yellowstone's caldera, or collapsed crater.

Glaciers, too, have left their mark, grinding down peaks and scouring out valleys and, on the northern plains, forcing the Missouri River to abandon its original route to Hudson Bay. Receding, the glacial ice left immense primeval lakes such as Bonneville and Lahontan, the forebears of today's Great Salt Lake in Utah. Their stranded blocks of ice in northern Idaho formed Lake Pend Oreille (pronounced "pon-der-ray"), with a depth of 1,200 feet. World War II submarine crews trained here.

Rising to heights of 10,000 to 14,000 feet, with Colorado's Mount Elbert at 14,432 feet the highest peak of all, the Rocky Mountains are divided into four general provinces—the southern, Wyoming Basin, middle, and northern. There are many ranges with many names—the Sawtooths, the Uintas, the Wind River, the San Juans, the Bitterroots—all born of the same oppositional forces, all splendid.

CLIMATE AND PLANT LIFE

Though it is landlocked and largely semiarid, the Pacific Ocean figures mightily in the region's climate. Air arrives over the western seaboard laden with moisture, nudged along by prevailing westerly winds. Square in the path of this flow are range upon range of mountains, the majority of which lie on a north-south axis.

Indian paintbrush, Seedskadee NWR, Wyoming

Missouri River and cottonwoods, Charles M. Russell NWR, Montana

Forced upward along their western slopes, the air cools to dewpoint and drops its water as rain or snow. Descending the eastern side, the air is much drier. Lands immediately to the east lie in a "rain shadow," a dry zone created by the moisture-grabbing mountains. The phenomenon plays itself out over the region's greatly varied topography, creating locally varied climates and weather patterns, often in close proximity to one another.

Architects of weather, mountains figure prominently in the region's plant life as well. Snow accumulates in the highest ranges five to eight months of the year. In spring it is released in torrents, filling creeks that rush downslope to make ever larger rivers, which curl and wind like tendrils across semiarid valleys and plains. Miles away, across lands receiving just 6 to 13 inches of precipitation yearly, a life-giving pulse of mountain water arrives in late spring and early summer. The result is beautiful and poignant, a defining image of the region: a rolling expanse of thirsty beige earth patterned in gray-greens of sagebrush, yucca, and juniper; and, rising up along the watercourse, a verdant belt of willows, swaying grass, and a few stately cottonwoods.

Any given mountain will encompass a series of distinct realms of plant life, each favoring a particular combination of soil, elevation, moisture, sun, and shade. The vertical distribution of these "life zones," which in a span of 10,000 feet may range from prairie to alpine tundra, represents a natural diversity that on level ground would require more than 1,000 miles of latitudinal change. Grasslands, typically shortgrass prairie, occupy the lowest reaches. Moving upslope, the region's marvelously varied shrublands appear—first and foremost sagebrush, a climax community in many areas—but also bitterbrush and rabbit brush and salt-tolerant species such as greasewood and saltbush. Higher yet are the mountain shrublands of chokecherry, curly-leafed mountain mahogany, juniper, and others. Grasses and wildflowers are associated with all of these varieties.

Coniferous forests are of two major types, montane and subalpine. The former is dominated by ponderosa pine and Douglas fir, with aspen a major component in some areas. The subalpine fir is a fixture of the latter, the highest-elevation forest of the region; it begins at elevations of 7,000 feet or higher and reaches to the treeline, which generally ends at 10,000 feet. Beyond the trees lies alpine tundra, rocky expanses of ground-hugging shrubs, mosses, and wildflowers.

Fulfilling their historic mission of preserving migratory bird habitat, the region's NWRs by and large encompass water, and so occupy valleys and basins. A few, however, include some coniferous forest. Many feature opportunities to see the workings of shrub communities, wetland complexes, and the lush mixture of water-loving deciduous trees and shrubs that hold sway along river and stream corridors.

WILDLIFE

From its wide-open plains to rugged high country, the Rocky Mountain region is home to a magnificent array of wild creatures: large (occasionally very large) and small; feathered, scaled, and furred. There is much to appreciate.

Hoofprints appear at all elevations. The deer family is well represented, with both mule deer and white-tailed deer abundant; its two largest members, the moose and elk, thrive here as well. A deerlike hoofprint on the prairie belongs to the pronghorn, though it is neither deer, goat, nor antelope. Swift, graceful runners with superb vision, pronghorn are the sole survivors of a long-extinct family. The mountain goat and bighorn sheep inhabit the highest, most rugged areas; they leave hoofprints, too, when they're not capering on bare rock. The largest hoofprints of all belong to the American bison. A herd of 400 or so roams the enclosure of the National Bison Range; herds also occupy Yellowstone and Grand Teton national parks.

Deer and other small mammals—Ord's kangaroo rat, desert cottontail, black-tailed and white-tailed prairie dogs—form a rich prey base for wild cats and dogs. Largely unseen, the mountain lion, which on average consumes one deer

Pronghorn, National Bison Range, Montana

per week, is widespread across the region. Its cousin the bobcat is also present and equally elusive. Joining the opportunistic coyote and red fox today is the gray wolf. Reintroduced to Yellowstone National Park and Idaho in 1995-96, packs are still becoming established; loners or pairs are drifting through the forests of Greater Yellowstone, trailing elk and deer and roaming farther afield to assess new areas for occupancy.

Declining in many areas today, the region's native cutthroat trout are biodiversity incarnate. There are many species and several subspecies, as well. A sampling of species names—Snake River, Colorado, Lahontan, Rio Grande, Yellowstone—is an important reminder of evolution; over thousands of years, each has evolved in accord with a specific

Western tanager

watershed or river basin. Arctic grayling, another native, inhabit a few alpine lakes and streams, including those on Red Rock Lakes NWR.

Birds fill marshlands, prairies, and forests with color and song. Grasslands and canyons are the haunts of such raptors as the golden eagle and prairie falcon. The trumpeter swan, sandhill crane, and American white pelican grace rivers and valleys. A tremendous array of shorebirds and waterfowl nest or migrate through, following the Pacific and Central flyways. Lovely songbirds— the chestnut-collared longspur, lazuli bunting, western tanager, MacGillivray's warbler—await visitors at many refuges, along with prolific colonies of wading birds, terns, gulls, and others.

THEN AND NOW

What do global capitalism, population growth, and a couple of two-ounce songbirds have in common? The birds—a Baird's sparrow, say, and black-and-white warbler, both ground nesters—inhabit native prairie and pockets of woodlands on a ranch of modest proportions, between 1,500 to 3,000 acres. Imported beef from Mexico and other countries keeps U.S. domestic prices below the cost of production. Hard pressed to make a living, the landowner has a new alternative: Subdivide the ranch into small parcels, each selling for a lucrative sum. Out go the cows, in come the homes. End of songbird habitat.

Of the many threats to natural diversity, none is as lasting as the conversion of open land to housing, be it trailer park or million-dollar summer residence. Degraded pasture or streamside woodlands can be restored—the refuge system has been doing it successfully for 80 years—but land lost to civilization is lost for

Rocky Mountain bighorn sheep

good. If ever there were doubts about the importance of private lands in conserving the region's wildlife, the past decade has erased them. The Rocky Mountain region is growing steadily, and land values continue to rise accordingly.

Much of the growth is focused on the margins of the most intact natural areas: Colorado's Rocky Mountain Front, Utah's Wasatch Mountains, the Flathead and Gallatin valleys of Montana, which respectively adjoin Glacier and Yellowstone national parks. Any piece of real estate claiming to border public lands is stamped with a wildly inflated price and sells quickly. The result, increasingly, is the confinement of wild species to "islands" of natural areas bounded by roads and population centers. The phenomenon occurs on scales spanning hundreds of miles or a few hundred acres. Even if that hypothetical ranch remains in business, its value to wildlife is sharply diminished should adjoining lands be developed. Many songbirds are no different from wolves in terms of having a threshold need for security. When they lose it in one area, they leave to find it elsewhere.

Many of the region's best-known fauna—elk, bison, grizzly bears, bighorn sheep, mountain lions, and now wolves—demand immense tracts of land; several species require land of two distinct types, one for summer, the other for winter. A visit to the National Elk refuge in glitzy Jackson Hole, Wyoming, between November and March will put the issue in focus. The town—and not a very large town at that—has consumed 75 percent of the winter range needed by one of the world's largest elk herds.

A concept now being promoted by a few conservationists involves linking natural "islands" via a series of protected corridors. These would provide the larger, nomadic species a measure of security as they roam. Most important, the plan would allow isolated groups of like animals to intermingle, and presumably to breed, amplifying the exchange of genetic information—a vital element for the long-term viability of these species.

The time-honored environmental issues of the region—alteration of river ecology by dams, poorly considered timber harvests and grazing practices on some federal lands, loss of wetlands and riparian areas—remain alive, with many committed people and organizations fighting the good fight. Economics is the elusive adversary. Traditional land uses today are difficult for people whose farms or ranches are already paid for. Newcomers who might desire to follow this path—to balance stewardship of a living landscape with a modest income obtained through grazing or cropping a portion of it, while carrying a mortgage—will find there is virtually no way to do so without enormous assets to begin with. Across the region, the average ranch owner is in his or her late fifties or early sixties. The "graying" of this generation, coupled with the dismal prospects facing the next, suggests that the pace of change across the Rocky Mountain states will not abate any time soon.

REFUGES AND THE CHANGING LANDSCAPE

It's possible to see birds, mammals, flowers, and trees on a great variety of lands, public and private; yet the difference between a landscape pulling double duty for human needs and one maintained solely for natural diversity is often dramatic, even to the untrained eye. There is more of everything, and more kinds of everything on the refuges.

Conserving plant and animal species on refuges today is a sometimes labor-intensive process. The word "management" has negative implications for some

Yellow-bellied marmot

Wetlands and snow-capped mountains, Alamosa–Monte Vista NWR Complex, Colorado

environmentalists, but as habitats are lost elsewhere, human intervention becomes necessary to mimic or maintain natural processes in the long run. Many of the refuges featured in this book are engaged in such work, the most typical of which is manipulating water levels in natural or constructed wetlands. Water is the West's most precious resource, with a host of interests competing for it.

Refuge staffs today possess a stunning amount of knowledge regarding the often highly specific needs of one species versus another. With knowledge comes new opportunities and new dilemmas. A change in water levels of a few inches will transform a wet meadow of spike rush and sedge into a mosaic of cattail and bulrush; avocets and godwits prefer one type of environment, ruddy ducks another, white-faced ibis something else. Which species or group receives the benefits? What is the underlying rationale? There is almost never a single, easy answer. Visit with refuge managers and staff, who in most cases understand the most intricate ecological proceedings on their lands.

CONCLUSION

Come and see the country—by foot or canoe, in winter or summer. Amble. Poke around. The opportunities for solitude and natural discoveries are great.

Several refuges in this guide are immense and rise to the level of wilderness—one would have to visit them every week for years to become thoroughly

acquainted. At these sites, pick one or two interesting areas, whatever your schedule allows, rather than driving hither and yon to see it all at once. Some smaller refuges are perfectly suited to a shorter visit on a travel day between the region's many national parks and monuments.

Enjoy.

Alamosa–Monte Vista NWR Complex
Alamosa, Colorado

Spring snow melt, Alamosa–Monte Vista NWR Complex

Life in the pastoral San Luis Valley hangs by a thread; a cold, clear, watery thread. The neighboring mountains are usually generous, saving it up all winter to fill the rivers in spring. Then the pumping begins. Water is pulled out, sprayed over the vast fields of potatoes, carrots, cabbage, and barley that are used in the brewing of Colorado's own Coors beer. Water is pulled out also to flood the meadows, marshes, and sloughs of Alamosa–Monte Vista NWR Complex, just in time for the arrival of shorebirds and ducks and egrets. Water. Every living thing here needs it—turns green from it, laps at it, swims in it, eats what grows in it—save for the pocket mice and horned lizards, the saltbush and greasewood. Everybody wants it—the refuge needs it to preserve a shred of the valley's wetland life; farmers and ranchers need it for their livelihoods. Even people who don't live in Colorado want the San Luis Valley's water.

By midsummer the refuge is dry as a stone. Scattered thunderstorms occur frequently in the hot months, but, all told, the area's total annual precipitation is around 8 inches. The Rio Grande flows weakly, used up. The refuge wetlands are drying or dry. Out on the crop fields, the pumping continues. Water.

HISTORY

Human occupancy of the San Luis Valley reaches back 11,000 or so years. Only a small portion of the refuge complex has been examined for cultural resources; ancient campsites and projectile points have been discovered on-site, and many more sites and artifacts of Clovis culture have turned up on private land in the valley. The Ute Indians prospered here in the years preceding European settlement.

Following the Mexican War of 1848, San Luis Valley became U.S. territory, and development proceeded steadily. Mining, ranching, and farming have all had their time here. Monte Vista NWR was established in 1953, Alamosa in 1962. The refuges were combined into one complex in 1979.

Agriculture has grown significantly in the valley since the 1970s. Along with reducing wetlands and other habitats, it has drastically altered the valley's water regime. Virtually nothing here functions naturally today. Large-scale irrigation has depleted river flows; spring flooding along the Rio Grande, which formerly recharged wetlands on the Alamosa unit and elsewhere, has been sharply curtailed. On Monte Vista refuge, a spring-fed stream, Spring Creek, ceased to flow in the early 1980s as a result of groundwater depletion, killing off a resident trout community.

To combat wetland loss, the refuge took a page from agriculture: It got into the irrigation business. Alamosa refuge owns two dams on the Rio Grande. Utilizing canals and diversion pumps at both units to harvest spring runoff, refuge staff oversee the flooding of expansive man-made and natural basins. Recent proposals to "export" water from the valley for municipal use in other portions of Colorado and even Albuquerque, New Mexico, have elicited staunch opposition from all quarters, including the refuge and area farmers. For the moment anyway, some of the usual disputes seem inconsequential, reinforcing the old western adage, "whiskey is for drinking, water for fighting."

GETTING THERE

Monte Vista NWR: From the city of Alamosa, travel west on paved route 8-S for about 12 mi., turning right (north) onto County Rd. 15; refuge headquarters and the auto-tour route are 0.75 mi. ahead, on the right.

Alamosa NWR: From the city of Alamosa, travel east on US Hwy. 160 for 4 mi., turning right (south) onto El Rancho Lane; continue to refuge headquarters and Visitor Center.

■ **SEASON:** Open year-round.

■ **HOURS:** Refuge open daylight hours. The Visitor Contact Station at Monte Vista is staffed by volunteers and is open 7:30 a.m.–4 weekdays and closed on weekends. Outdoor information kiosks contain brochures for visitors to use when the Visitor Contact Station is closed.

■ **FEES:** None.

■ **ADDRESS:** 9383 El Rancho Lane, Alamosa, CO 81101

■ **TELEPHONE:** 719/589-4021

TOURING ALAMOSA–MONTE VISTA

■ **BY AUTOMOBILE:** Alamosa: A 3.5-mile self-guided auto tour will open in the summer of 2000; the unpaved refuge road to Bluff Overlook area provides year-round access.

Monte Vista: Refuge roads provide good year-round access. Included are a 4-mile self-guided auto-tour route, as well as three county roads, two of which are paved.

■ **BY FOOT:** Alamosa: Waking the refuge is permitted year-round on a 2-mile trail originating at the refuge Visitor Center and along unpaved refuge roads; short walks are permitted around Bluff Overlook. A walking trail among refuge wet meadows is in the blueprint stage.

Monte Vista: Hiking is permitted year-round along county roads—no foot travel is permitted on the auto-tour route. The security of birds—particularly that of sandhill cranes—is a high priority here.

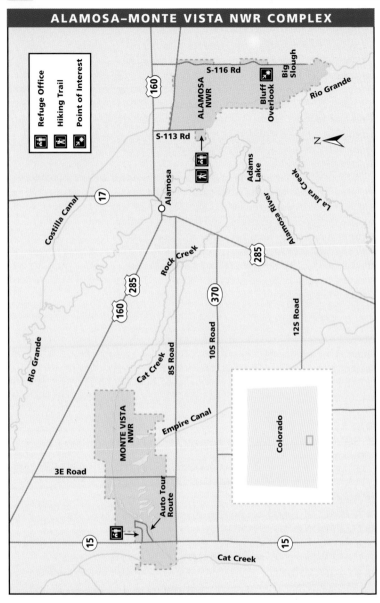

ALAMOSA–MONTE VISTA NWR COMPLEX

Refuge Office
Hiking Trail
Point of Interest

S-116 Rd
Big Slough
160
ALAMOSA NWR
Bluff Overlook
Rio Grande
S-113 Rd
N
Adams Lake
Alamosa
17
Atamosa River
La Jara Creek
Rock Creek
285
Costilla Canal
285
160
370
285
Rio Grande
Cat Creek
8S Road
10S Road
125 Road
MONTE VISTA NWR
Empire Canal
Colorado
3E Road
Auto Tour Route
15
15
Cat Creek

■ **BY BICYCLE:** Biking is permitted along county roads at Monte Vista only.

■ **BY CANOE, KAYAK, OR BOAT:** Not permitted.

WHAT TO SEE

■ **LANDSCAPE AND CLIMATE** Encompassing some 8,000 square miles at a mean elevation of 7,600 feet, this is thought to be the largest alpine valley in the world. Both refuge units lie within the San Luis Valley, and two mountain ranges form its boundaries. On the western skyline are the jagged San Juans, with the Sangre De Cristo range to the east. Both include peaks in excess of 13,000 feet; Crestone Peak, one of the jewels of the Sangre De Cristos, soars to 14,294 feet.

The valley floor is desert, and receives six or seven inches of precipitation annually; with a growing season of 95 days. The mountains, which collect snow seven to eight months of the year, release meltwater in the springtime, which creates many rivers. One such river is the storied Rio Grande, which meanders across the southern reaches of the valley and forms the western boundary of the Alamosa unit. Water has come and gone for eons, but a sizable portion has accrued beneath the valley floor in the form of two aquifers and numerous Artesian wells, several of which are scattered across the refuge complex.

Prior to settlement, the Rio Grande was free to change course on the basis of cyclical fluctuations in snowmelt and climate. Several thousand years ago it vacated a large stretch of historic channel. Southwest winds picked up the dried riverbed and deposited it at the base of the Sangre De Cristos, forming 39 square miles of sand dunes, the tallest (at 700 feet above the valley floor) in North America. Located about 40 miles northeast of the refuge complex, this area is preserved today as Great Sand Dunes National Monument.

■ PLANT LIFE AND HABITATS The Rio Grande no longer inundates its floodplain with the frequency, volume, or velocity it once did. Before human intervention, *volume* refilled riverine wetlands, most notably at Alamosa. *Velocity* served to flush out calcium and salt buildups that accrue naturally in these very saline soils. Once a more or less annual event, a good spring washout now occurs once *every 4 years*. There would be few wetlands here today without assistance from people. Indeed, it is amazing what people can do as substitutes for nature. By directing water into one or another area, refuge staff can foster salt flats, salt grasses, and eventually greasewood stands, or eliminate salt to encourage cattails, rushes, and sedges. Across both units, but especially at Monte Vista, some amount of back-and-forth between saltwater and freshwater plant life has occurred naturally over many years. It's a pliable landscape. Given the loss of wetland habitat throughout the valley, restoring and creating a variety of wetlands remain the priorities.

Wetlands Each spring, water from the Rio Grande is diverted into Alamosa's 9,000 acres of natural sloughs, shallow basins, oxbows, and wet meadows. A similar process occurs at Monte Vista. Though largely man-made, its wetlands are very successful. A 1996 monograph cited these 8,000 acres—mosaics of marsh, open water, and wet meadows—as among the most productive duck nesting areas in North America. Baltic rush and spike rush are key emergent species in wet meadows, which begin the year soggy and steadily dry. Semi-permanent wetlands offer open water and belts of cattail with bulrush, both hard- and softstem; most hold water all year.

Regardless of type, the secret to wetland productivity remains a natural one. Often, the healthiest wet-

Snowy egret

lands are those that go from wet to damp to dry each year; this annual "boom and bust" cycle yields the greatest abundance of invertebrates and other aquatic life that feed shorebirds, ducks, and other species. In this climate, little human intervention is necessary to assist wetlands in drying out.

Salt desert shrublands "Uplands" is a suspect term in the Rio Grande floodplain, where a major grade is all of 2 feet. A rise of just 2 to 6 inches changes everything; freshwater plants like sedges and cattail vanish, and the salt-lovers—

White-faced ibis

greasewood, with an understory of salt grass—appear. Scattered mosaics of this type are common at Monte Vista, and the shorebirds love it. With its fleshy, elongated leaves of vivid green, greasewood looks like it arrived from another planet. Four-winged saltbush, another resident of the salt pans, is pretty strange-looking, too. Both are members of the goosefoot family, a collection of tough, pungent-smelling herbs; native plants, they're toxic to livestock if eaten in sufficient quantities. Greasewood grows in thickets to a height of 5 feet or more; saltbush grows lower to the ground. Several varieties of rabbit brush occur in the uplands as well. A close relative of sagebrush, it tolerates some salt, though less than the shrubs mentioned above. Rabbit brush produces attractive yellow blooms in late summer through fall.

Growing boldly where most plants fear to tread, salt-desert shrublands occupy the northern third of Alamosa and roughly 15 percent of Monte Vista. Understories are varied; Indian ricegrass and salt grass dominate in different areas; wild rose and several asters, along with goldenrod, fireweed, locoweed, and giant bee plant, are also present. The slender spider flower, an uncommon species, is found here.

Riparian areas Varying from dense thickets to open, parklike stands, riparian woodlands of willow and cottonwood occur mostly along the Rio Grande in Alamosa. Alamosa's are thickest, with many mature willows, including sandbar and other species, bounding the Rio Grande and its many old meanders, oxbows, and sloughs. Mature cottonwoods are scattered here, too, as well as at Monte Vista at old homestead sites, graceful figures often standing alone amid the wet meadows and marshes. Outside refuge boundaries, riparian woodlands across the Rio Grande floodplain have been degraded by livestock grazing. The altered water cycle here has affected willow and cottonwood reproduction. Today's woodlands are even-aged, with minimal new recruits. When Spring Creek lost its spring on

Monte Vista, the willows died away. Refuge management at this time is beginning restoration work on the creek, which also had been channelized while in private hands. Plans call for reestablishing meanders on the stream and for possible reestablishment of sandbar willow and narrowleaf cottonwood.

■ ANIMAL LIFE

Birds The larger wetlands of Monte Vista feature small islands, which in spring and summer are nesting sites for an array of splendid birds. One of the state's largest snowy egret rookeries is here, with large numbers of black-crowned night-herons and American bitterns. Another site deep in bulrush is home to Colorado's largest nesting colony of white-faced ibis.

The wet meadows and open waters of both units are alive with waterfowl and their broods—the ruddy duck, lesser scaup, redhead, and northern pintail are easily seen, as are three species of teal. The American avocet and Wilson's phalarope are the most commonly seen shorebirds, though many others may be hanging around, especially along the mudflats and shallows of the Rio Grande—among them, the pectoral sandpiper, long-billed curlew, black-bellied plover, and black-necked stilt. These occur more readily during migratory seasons.

The marquee event here is the seasonal appearance of sandhill cranes. The entire Rocky Mountain population of greater sandhills—some 22,000 birds, plus the odd whooping crane or two—gather at San Luis Valley in mid-March in preparation for their northward journey. The sight of these huge concentrations of tall, graceful birds in what amounts to a traffic bottleneck is truly amazing.

Songbird diversity at Alamosa is somewhat limited, if also a bit unusual in that it sometimes involves two completely different habitats bumping up against each other in close quarters. Commonly seen species include the sage thrasher, western wood pewee, savannah sparrow, American goldfinch, yellow-rumped warbler, pine sisken, and long-billed marsh wren. Sighted occasionally are the loggerhead shrike, black-headed and blue grosbeaks, Bullock's oriole, and black-throated sparrow.

Greater sandhill cranes, Alamosa–Monte Vista NWR Complex

Mammals Though all but invisible, a fascinating group of mice inhabit the complex. Three species of pocket mouse are common: the olive-backed, Apache, and silky; all are handsome, two-toned mice well adapted to this climate: They drink no water, instead drawing moisture from the many seeds they eat. The western harvest mouse is common, as is the western jumping mouse, a largish mouse with a lengthy tail, yellow sides, and a dark band down the center of its back. This species, bounding 3 to 5 feet when startled, may be seen in daylight, foraging around shrubs. Also here is the most predatory of all mice, the northern grasshopper mouse.

Other little chiselers are more readily seen or heard. The least chipmunk, white-tailed prairie dog, and Ord's kangaroo rat are all abundant. Four rabbit species are here—black- and white-tailed jackrabbits and desert and Nuttall's cottontails. Coyote, badger, and long-tailed weasel, all common, prey on these creatures. Rare mammals passing through the refuge complex include mountain lion, black bear, and bobcat. Don't expect to catch a glimpse of them.

Mule deer and pronghorn are often seen here; in winter, a large elk herd of 600 or so migrates to Monte Vista from mountains to the west. Viewing them is popular along Highway 15, and, through a partnership, the refuge has just secured funding for three large visitor turnouts along this route. Other common mammals include beaver, along with the usual opportunists—porcupine, raccoon, and striped skunk. Seven species of bat move through the complex on their migrations to and from nursery sites.

Reptiles and amphibians The short-horned lizard lives here, a plump little animal with a headdress of spines. It's present on both complexes and active in

Porcupine

daylight, spring through fall, though more readily seen on lands immediately adjacent to the refuges. At Alamosa, the bull snake occurs in a wide variety of areas, from wetland margins to drier, hotter uplands. Monte Vista hosts the western rattlesnake. The western terrestrial garter snake inhabits both units, usually near water.

Many frogs and toads are here. The Great Plains and Plains spadefoot toads favor the shrublands, while the Woodhouse's toad prefers wetter sites. The striped chorus frog, western chorus frog, bullfrog, and northern leopard frog may all be heard in spring and early summer in marshes and wet meadows.

ACTIVITIES

■ **CAMPING:** No camping or swimming is allowed on the refuge.

■ **WILDLIFE OBSERVATION:** On the whole, spring (March–May) and fall (September–November) are the most productive and enjoyable times to visit. The spectacular sandhill crane event is easily accessible for viewing by parked vehicles—the birds are virtually right outside a visitor's car window. They pass through twice a year: in spring and again in fall. Winter brings reliable sightings of bald and golden eagles, along with many rough-legged hawks. A new 3.5-mile self-guided auto tour is under construction at Alamosa and should be completed by the summer of 2000.

> **HUNTING AND FISHING**
> **Ducks, coots, geese, cottontail**, and **jackrabbits** can be hunted Oct. through Jan., but check on breaks during this period when hunting is not permitted. In the fall, there are specific weeks when hunting for **doves, snipes**, and **pheasants** is allowed. There is no fishing on the refuge.

■ **PHOTOGRAPHY:** Experience, patience, and telephoto lenses are necessary for images of nesting birds. There are terrific opportunities for landscapes and scenic images of the valley, with old log outbuildings and bovines adding charming touches. Permission is needed to get close to nesting birds on Monte Vista.

■ **HIKES AND WALKS:** At Alamosa, dedicated walkers should follow the trail along the Rio Grande. It's a 2-mile round-trip along the river, traversing willow thickets and shallow river flats, with opportunities to sight waterfowl and snowy egrets, as well as shorebirds.

■ **SEASONAL EVENTS:** March (midmonth): Annual Monte Vista Crane Festival, one of Colorado's best-attended wildlife viewing galas. The fun includes many speakers, displays, and guided tours of Monte Vista for up-close viewing of thousands of sandhill cranes and other species. October: National Wildlife Refuge Week, at Monte Vista.

■ **PUBLICATIONS:** Refuge visitor brochure; bird and mammal checklists; *Directory of Birding and Nature Festivals,* with information on the Monte Vista Crane Festival.

Arapaho NWR
Walden, Colorado

Arapaho Valley at 8,000 feet, Arapaho NWR

Square in the heart of the Rockies, 24,804-acre Arapaho NWR is a place to feel a bit light-headed. The floor of this unspoiled valley, crisscrossed with cold, clear-running rivers and streams, is at 8,000 feet—a height at which many mountains top out. The peaks and ridges here keep going, and going, bounding the valley on all sides save the north. Locked in winter much of the year, Arapaho, like the rest of the valley, is first to be released; its willows and sedge meadows come to life, blue flag iris bloom, and by mid-May a wealth of Rocky Mountain fauna, from shorebirds to moose, are here in abundance.

HISTORY

Before the time of European settlement, North Park, as the local area is called, was the "cow lodge" and "bull pen" to the Ute Indians, who camped here in the summers to chase down herds of bison. The southern Cheyenne and Arapaho at various times were associated with the region as well. North Park's value for cattle was established by the 1880s, when herds from the Front Range along Fort Collins were driven over Lulu Pass, near present-day Cameron Pass, to graze the valley through the summer. Coal mining and timber harvesting, dwindling today, were important economic activities through the latter half of the 1800s.

Arapaho NWR was established in 1967, in part to offset losses of migratory bird habitat in the Northern Plains. Visitation is modest, about 6,000 people per year, perhaps due to isolation and elevation.

GETTING THERE

From Laramie, WY, on I-80, travel southwest on WY 230 for 41 mi. to Colorado, where the road continues as CO 127; drive 9 mi. to the junction with CO 125; continue south 13 mi. through the town of Walden, onto the refuge.

From Granby, CO, on US 40, travel north 56 mi. on CO 125 to the refuge.

When they are completed, the refuge headquarters and Visitor Center will be located just east of CO 125 on County Rd. 32.

■ **SEASON:** Open spring, summer, fall.

■ **HOURS:** The refuge is open during daylight hours; the refuge headquarters is open weekdays 7 a.m.–4:30 p.m.

■ **FEES:** None.

■ **ADDRESS:** P.O. Box 457, Walden, CO 80480

■ **TELEPHONE:** 970/723-8202

TOURING ARAPHAHO

■ **BY AUTOMOBILE:** Good seasonal access. All refuge roads, including a 6-mile interpreted loop tour, are open spring through fall unless posted otherwise or closed due to weather; all roads close in winter except for the main road to the refuge headquarters. Three county roads either bound refuge land or pass through it.

■ **BY FOOT:** No bushwacking. Walking and hiking are limited to a half-mile interpretive trail and to refuge roads (including the auto-tour route). Permission may be granted to explore other areas on foot; contact refuge staff prior to your visit.

■ **BY BICYCLE:** Biking is not permitted on the refuge.

■ **BY CANOE, KAYAK, OR BOAT:** Boating is not permitted on the refuge.

WHAT TO SEE

■ **LANDSCAPE AND CLIMATE** Arapaho refuge lies in a large intermountain glacial basin, in a high desert valley of considerable elevation. The valley is bounded to the west by the Park Range, which includes the Continental Divide at elevations of 10,000 to 12,000 feet, and to the east by the stately Medicine Bow Mountains; Rabbit Ears Range rises to the south, crowned by Parkview Mountain at 12,296 feet. These mountains capture immense amounts of snowfall 6 to 8 months of the year—more than 300 inches annually. The meltwater from these mountains feeds numerous streams and rivers, including the Illinois, which meanders broadly across the refuge en route to its meeting with the Michigan River, north of Walden; the Michigan, in turn, meets the beautiful North Platte River just north of Cowdrey.

The valley continues as a stronghold for agrarian culture; irrigated pasturelands of non-native grasses and alfalfa are grown for livestock, primarily cattle, using water from area streams. Drier upland areas, most of which maintain native grassland communities, are also grazed seasonally. But rain and snowfall occur over the *moun-*

Prickly pear cactus

tains, with very little left for the refuge and valley—just 9.5 inches of precipitation collect annually on the refuge.

Winters are lengthy and windy—temperatures between November and March average 20 degrees Fahrenheit—while summer daytime temperatures average 85 degrees. Refuge lands are frost-free just 45 days per year.

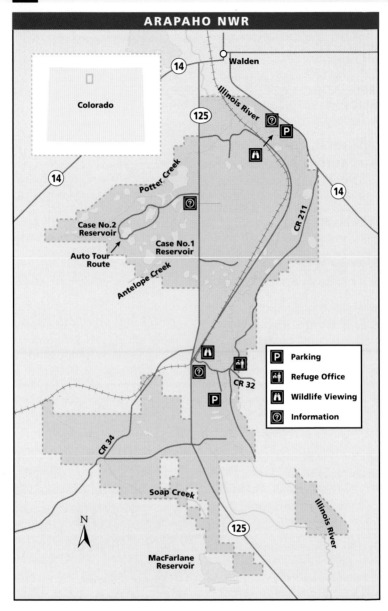

■ PLANT LIFE AND HABITATS

Wetlands Arapaho features 839 acres of pond and marsh habitat. Concentrated heavily in the northern half of the refuge, these pools are fed by the Illinois River via old irrigation ditches. For the most part, ponds fill in spring and steadily diminish through summer, with some going dry in fall. Cattails are scant, owing to the elevation; more widespread are Baltic rush and carex sedge, with aquatic vegetation such as pondweed and milfoils.

Spread over 8,946 acres is a lush carpet of wet meadows, the dominant wetland habitat here. Irrigated to maintain their value to wildlife, these lands are a mosaic of sedges, rushes, and nonnative timothy grass, with pockets of forbs such as wild iris and wild chives. The smallest wetland type—some 200 acres of riparian thickets along the Illinois River—is among the most critical in this essentially desert landscape. Willow is by far the dominant species of these streamside corridors; in all, 11 species grow here, including mountain and plainleaf. A few old cottonwood trees are present as well, vestiges of the days when the refuge was a working ranch; ranchers from that era introduced the nonnative cottonwoods to the area.

Arid lands About 12,860 acres of sagebrush grasslands unroll over the knolls, slopes, and other upland areas of Arapaho. Thriving in areas with less than 12 inches of annual precipitation and cooler temperatures (which tend to come above 6,000 feet), sagebrush does well here—mountain big sage and Wyoming sage are the dominant varieties. Standing 2 feet or so in height, mature sagebrush makes excellent shade in summer and breaks the wind in winter, meeting two very important needs of wildlife in this harsh environment. Other specialists of the high desert, such as greasewood and rabbit brush, are present in smaller amounts. Understory species include needlegrass, some fescues and wheatgrasses, along with snakeweed, prickly pear cactus, and phlox.

■ ANIMAL LIFE

Birds Once as common as its namesake shrub, the sage grouse is steadily declining across the West; chances are good it will be a candidate for federal endangered species listing in the near future. Sage grouse remain at Arapaho, their numbers as ever subject to cyclical trends, but refuge staff note that peak populations no longer reach the peaks of earlier years.

The white-faced ibis, another species with an uncertain future, began nesting here in 1998 and '99; the refuge is hopeful that this trend will continue. The American avocet, Wilson's phalarope, and willet are common nesting shorebirds; rare to uncommon are the spotted sandpiper and Virginia rail. A black-crowned night-heron rookery is busy in summer; other nesting species include the black tern, yellow-headed blackbird, sora, and a lively contingent of waterfowl—lesser scaup, gadwall, green-winged and cinnamon teal, and ruddy duck, among several others.

The dry uplands offer chances to sight a sage thrasher or vesper sparrow, or perhaps to hear the cricketlike trill of a rock wren. The burrowing and short-eared owls are present in limited numbers, as are the lark bunting and green-tailed towhee; the horned lark, mountain bluebird, and rufous hummingbird are common.

Arapaho is a good site for raptors. The golden eagle, northern harrier, prairie falcon, and Swain-

Displaying sage grouse, Arapaho NWR

White-tailed prairie dog, Arapaho NWR

son's hawk are frequently seen; the peregrine falcon and bald eagle make occasional appearances.

Mammals This valley features the highest concentration of moose in Colorado, and the Arapaho refuge is a terrific place to look for them. Reintroduced to the region in the late 1970s, these are the Shiras subspecies, a slightly smaller cousin of the massive eastern moose. It's all relative, of course; a moose is still a moose, North America's largest deer. You're most likely to see one (not a herd) grazing in wet places, perhaps knee-deep in water.

A more recent reintroduction is also succeeding. River otters, released outside refuge boundaries by the Colorado Division of Wildlife, have taken hold and are now a constant if elusive presence at Arapaho. Winter drives a large herd of elk— 700 to 800 animals—onto the refuge, where they feed heavily in both sagebrush grasslands and irrigated meadows; mule deer appear as well, in small numbers. Other mammals seen with regularity include the pronghorn antelope, beaver, and muskrat. The white-tailed prairie dog is abundant, sharing its colonial space with Richardson's ground squirrels. The white-tailed jackrabbit, coyote, long-tailed weasel, least chipmunk, and badger are all common; seen occasionally are the golden-mantled ground squirrel, yellow-bellied marmot, red fox, Nuttall's cottontail, porcupine, and ermine.

A PERFECT LITTLE BEAST Mountain lions, wolves, grizzly bears—the West's marquee predators have nothing on the northern grasshopper mouse. Though it weighs less than 2 ounces, this stout little mouse, colored gray-black or cinnamon-buff, hunts grasshoppers, beetles, even scorpions, and may kill other mice. It aggressively defends its young, even against people. Largely nocturnal, the little beast emits a long, high-pitched howl, with upraised snout and open mouth, not unlike a wolf. Arapaho NWR has documented the presence of northern grasshopper mice. Watch your step.

Reptiles and amphibians Given the high elevation, reptiles and amphibians are scant. But you can use your ears to find the striped chorus frog, wood frog, and northern leopard frog, or your eyes to search for the wandering garter snake, a rare species, and the tiger salamander.

Fish The Illinois River supports a varied fishery, with introduced rainbow, brown, and brook trout; other species include the long-nosed sucker, creek chub, fathead minnow, northern redbelly dace, and Johnny darter.

ACTIVITIES

■ **CAMPING:** No camping on the refuge; but camping opportunities are plentiful throughout the area, including the Lake John and Delaney Butte Lakes state wildlife areas to the west, and on Routt National Forest and federal Bureau of Land Management lands surrounding North Park.

■ **WILDLIFE OBSERVATION:** Visitors arriving earlier than May will likely contend with sloppy refuge roads of meltwater mud. A small herd of elk make forays onto the refuge year-round and may be seen very early or late in the morning or evening. May through October are prime months for viewing most birdlife; fall migration peaks between late September and early October; waterfowl and shorebirds begin nesting in early June.

■ **PHOTOGRAPHY:** Refuge birds are accustomed to traffic on the auto tour and are not especially skittish when a vehicle creeps past. June is the ideal month for images of waterfowl, shorebirds, and wading birds in their bright breeding plumage—the greening valley and its palisades of snow-capped peaks provide incomparable scenery, which lasts for another month.

■ **HIKES AND WALKS:** The half-mile refuge nature trail winds along the lovely Illinois River, with opportunities to sight moose, beaver, muskrat, and songbirds in the willow thickets. Walking the trail, keep an eye out for river otters. Another scenic overlook in the northeastern reaches of the refuge offers viewing of meadow and riparian areas.

HUNTING AND FISHING Big-game archery and firearm seasons are for pronghorn only. Hunted small game includes both **cottontail rabbit** and **jackrabbit**. Waterfowl opportunities include **ducks**, **coot**, **merganser**, as well as **Canada geese**. Upland birds and other migratory species hunted here are **sage grouse**, **common snipe**, **rail**, and **dove**.

The Illinois River supports **brown trout** and other cold-water species. The refuge is regularly closed to fishing between June 1 and Aug. 1 to allow for waterfowl nesting.

■ **SEASONAL EVENTS:** None.

■ **PUBLICATIONS:** Refuge brochure; auto-tour guide; checklist of vertebrates; a guide to year-round recreation in North Park is available through the refuge or by contacting the Walden Tourism Information Center at 970/723-4344.

Browns Park NWR
Maybell, Colorado

Ruffed grouse

Human-imposed boundaries and names mean little out here; it's all of a piece: sprawling plateaus; weathered sandstone in desert hues of soft yellows and golds; deep, toothy canyons carved by powerful rivers. Call it the high desert. Call it the soul of the West. The steep hills and long ridges are cloaked in dusky green expanses of shrublands and the black-green pockets of piñon pine and juniper; up higher are the cliffs and spires; down below, in the valleys, are the livelier greens of cottonwood, willow, and wetlands, where the most precious element of all—water—glistens in the sun.

This is the landscape encompassed by Browns Park NWR, a 13,445-acre refuge of great natural diversity and a rich human history. Located in the remote northwestern corner of Colorado, the nearest major settlement is Vernal, Utah, some 45 miles to the southwest. The refuge sits astride the Green River—just downstream is the stunning Canyon of Lodore, forming the northern boundary of Dinosaur National Monument, a 325-square-mile slice of canyonlands and fossil beds. Keep an eye on the gas gauge out here. Services and towns are widely dispersed—which means opportunities for exploration and natural wonders are unparalleled.

HISTORY

Browns Park features an unusually rich human history, the evidence of which extends back 1,700 years, when the Fremont Indian culture occupied the area. Petroglyphs, grain-storage buildings, and rock carvings from this era are all present on the refuge today. Tipi rings are remnants of later tribes such as the Shoshone Indians. Early settlers built Fort Davey Crockett here in 1837; not long after, the cattle-ranching era and California gold rush brought even more settlers and traders. With increased commerce, some of the West's best-known outlaws—Butch Cassidy and the Wild Bunch among them—roamed Browns Park and surrounding areas. Three state lines in close proximity were a boon to lawbreakers, who would flee jurisdictions and vanish in the rugged canyons.

Three National Historic Sites are found on the refuge, including the still intact Lodore Schoolhouse (1911). Efforts continue here to find the precise location of Fort Davey Crockett. Remains of the Two Bar Ranch, winter headquarters for an influential local rancher named Ora Haley, are here as well. Browns Park NWR was formally established in 1970, though its presence as a refuge dates from 1963.

GETTING THERE

From Craig, Colorado: Travel west on US 40 for 31 mi. to the town of Maybell; continue west on CO 318 for 50 mi. to refuge. From Vernal, Utah: Travel east on US 40 for 92 mi. to Maybell, Colorado, turning left/west onto CO 318; continue 50 mi. to refuge. From Rock Springs, Wyoming, on I-80: Travel south on US 191 for 106 mi. to Vernal, Utah, following directions above to refuge.

- **SEASON:** Open year-round.
- **HOURS:** Refuge headquarters and Visitor Center open weekdays, 8 a.m.– 4:30 p.m., year-round.
- **FEES:** None.
- **ADDRESS:** 1318 Hwy. 138, Maybell, CO 81640
- **TELEPHONE:** 970/365-3613

TOURING BROWNS PARK

- **BY AUTOMOBILE:** The 11-mile auto-tour route, open year-round and complete with interpretive stops, is the primary vehicular access. High-clearance or 4-wheel-drive vehicles are permitted along an unimproved road on the south side of the Green River.
- **BY FOOT:** Hiking is permitted year-round in all areas with the exception of refuge marshes, which are closed to visitors between March 1 and July 31. A developed birder's trail follows Beaver Creek near the refuge headquarters. An overlook of the Spitzie wetland area is found off the auto tour.
- **BY BICYCLE:** Bicycles are permitted along the gravel 11-mile auto-tour route and along the unimproved jeep road paralleling the south side of the Green River. Both provide good access to wildlife viewing and most habitats. Summers here are blazing hot, however, so bring along plenty of water.
- **BY CANOE, KAYAK, OR BOAT:** Floating the Green River is a memorable experience but, surprisingly,

Cinnamon teal

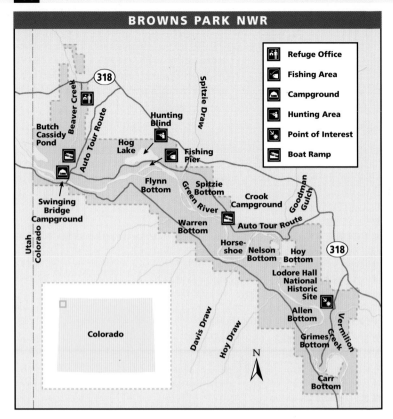

BROWNS PARK NWR

Refuge Office

Fishing Area

Campground

Hunting Area

Point of Interest

Boat Ramp

318

Spitzie Draw

Beaver Creek

Butch Cassidy Pond

Auto Tour Route

Hunting Blind

Hog Lake

Fishing Pier

Flynn Bottom

Spitzie Bottom

Green River

Crook Campground

Goodman Gulch

Swinging Bridge Campground

Warren Bottom

Auto Tour Route

Utah Colorado

Horse-shoe

Nelson Bottom

Hoy Bottom

318

Lodore Hall National Historic Site

Allen Bottom

Vermillion Creek

Colorado

Davis Draw

Hoy Draw

Grimes Bottom

N

Carr Bottom

not that popular here yet. Two boat ramps, one at each refuge campground, handle canoes and rafts. Shuttle services and canoe or boat rentals are available through the Browns Park store, 2 to 3 miles east of the refuge.

WHAT TO SEE

■ **LANDSCAPE AND CLIMATE** Browns Park lies within the Middle Rocky Mountain Province; the Continental Divide, with mountain peaks reaching 12,000 feet, is about 100 miles due west; to the east just 40 or so miles are the hulking Uinta Mountains of Utah. Refuge soils, climate, and animal and plant communities bear the influence of two even more vast physiographic regions—the parched Wyoming Basin to the north and the Colorado Plateau, a sprawling upthrust of semidesert extending from west-central Colorado into Utah, New Mexico, and Arizona.

Born in the Wind River mountains of Wyoming, the powerful Green River loops briefly through Colorado, bisecting the refuge, before turning back into Utah; on its long southward journey through these arid lands it has carved an endless series of dramatic, precipitious canyons.

Just 12 inches of precipitation fall at Browns Park annually, most of it arriving in winter. Summer temperatures often approach 100 degrees Fahrenheit; low temperatures in winter are well below freezing.

■ **PLANT LIFE AND HABITATS**
Open water The majestic Green River ambles pleasantly through the refuge,

flexing its muscles just downriver, in the jagged Canyon of Lodore. Controlled by several immense dams, the waters are meted out for agriculture, drinking water, and hydroelectricity. River ecology has been greatly altered as a result. Deep reservoirs create unnaturally cold water, rendering native fish such as the endangered Colorado squawfish—which may be seen here—incapable of spawning. Non-native species, including brown and rainbow trout, thrive in the colder river today. Dams have also eliminated seasonal flooding, which helps to rejuvenate stream-side forests and wetlands.

Wetlands Strung along the river are some 1,200 acres of wetlands, including deep water pools, shallower marshes with cattail and hardstem bulrush, and a series of wet meadows, comprising sedges and water-loving grasses. In lieu of seasonal flooding of the river, the refuge manipulates water cycles, pumping river water into some wetlands and drawing them down at other times of the year. Browns Park refuge would like to overhaul several wetland areas. Bulrush has overwhelmed some units, making them unproductive. Two more wetland units are infested with nonnative plants; management hopes to return these to their natural state as either seasonal wet meadows or grassland.

Forest Browns Park's bottomland (or riparian) forest borders the Green River and both Vermillion and Beaver creeks, a noteworthy 1,112 acres of deciduous greenery in a sun-scorched landscape. Dominant trees include Fremont's cotton-wood, narrow-leaf cottonwood, river birch, and sandbar willow. This forest has been in decline ever since the construction of Flaming Gorge Reservoir upstream; nonnative plants such as pepperweed and salt cedar have moved in.

Piñon-juniper woodlands stand in stark contrast to the deciduous forests along refuge waterways. A "pygmy forest" of Utah juniper and Colorado piñon pine occurs in small stands across the center of the refuge and more extensively along the southwestern boundary; a beautiful thicket of this high-desert forest type can also be explored near refuge headquarters.

Grasslands About 1,906 acres here feature a native intermountain grassland of alkali sacaton, salt grass, and Great Basin wild rye, along with nonnative cheat-grass, smooth brome, and pepperweed. Prescribed burning and chemical control

---

THE BUTCHER BIRD The shrublands of Browns Park are the favored haunts of the loggerhead shrike, a slender bird a bit smaller than a robin, colored dusky gray above and white below. The distinguishing feature of the loggerhead is its black mask—the ideal accessory for this diminutive hunter.

During the summer and fall the shrike captures large grasshoppers, mormon crickets, and other sizable insects, making good use of its beak, which is hooked at the end, much like a hawk's. When insects are in short supply, the shrike will pursue mice and voles. Upon capturing its prey, the bird flies to a nearby wire fence and impales the insect or rodent upon an upturned barb; there it hangs, along with other recent kills, as part of the shrike's food cache, a practice responsible for the bird's long-standing common name, "butcher bird."

The loggerhead shrike is listed as a species of management concern at Browns Park, and though it is doing quite well here—refuge staff project as many as 20 breeding pairs on the refuge—it has declined across much of its historic range.

are employed to keep exotics at bay. The Ute ladies' tresses orchid, a threatened wildflower that grows spiky white blooms, occurs along the Green River; other grassland flowers include Indian paintbursh, phlox, and globe mallow.

Arid lands Occupying nearly 8,000 acres of Browns Park is the signature plant community of the Colorado Plateau, the semidesert shrublands. Don't be fooled by its gnarled, desolate look—this mosaic of dense, low-growing shrubs, such as big sagebrush, rabbit brush, greasewood, and shadscale, pulses with life, from several fascinating birds to small mammals, lizards, and snakes. Beneath the shrubs is a sparse understory of Indian ricegrass, needle-and-thread, and sand dropseed. Also here is the tiny hedgehog cactus, which blooms scarlet in summer, and the prickly pear, with flowers that range from purple and rose to yellow and pink. Spiny hopsage and rabbit brush flower in spring.

■ **ANIMAL LIFE** Browns Park's splendidly diverse habitats make for an uncommonly rich wildlife community. Located on the Pacific Flyway, the refuge's riparian forests along the Green River and Beaver and Vermillion creeks are an essential stop for migrating songbirds, many of which cannot negotiate the semidesert lands of Utah, Colorado, and Wyoming. Instead, they follow the north-south corridors of the Green and Colorado rivers. The northern waterthrush, orange-crowned warbler, and warbling vireo are a few representative migrants here. Other nesters here are the yellow-billed cuckoo, western screech-owl, and Bullock's oriole.

Moose, beaver, and the northern river otter inhabit streamside forests and marshes at Browns Park. Moose are sighted regularly, otters less so, though parents and young have been seen, indicating a breeding population exists either on the refuge or nearby. As many as 30 bald eagles spend their winters in the riverside forests.

Refuge grasslands fill another critical seasonal need, in this case winter forage for a substantial mule deer and elk herd. Pushed into the valley by deep snow, between 400 and 1,200 elk may utilize the refuge; mule deer are seen year-round in grassland and shrubland areas, though their numbers skyrocket when food

Moose

becomes scarce elsewhere, with as many as 1,000 present each winter. A grassland devote, the pronghorn antelope exists here in small numbers.

Wetlands are the province of American bittern, yellow-headed blackbird, tiger salamander and Woodhouse's toad, and mink and muskrat. As many as 300 white-faced ibis visit the refuge during migration, and a dependable array of ducks nest on-site, including the cinnamon teal, northern pintail, and redhead. Also present in the marshes and wet meadows are five species of grebe, marsh wren, and a fine display of shorebirds, both resident and migrant.

A fair amount of the piñon-juniper forests here grow amid steeper, rocky terrain interspersed with cliffs. Refuge staff have documented 11 bat species on this site, including both the Townsend's big-eared bat and pallid bat. Peregrine falcons nest near the refuge in this terrain and are regularly observed hunting the

Tiger salamander

marshes spring through fall. The golden eagle, piñon jay, prairie falcon, cliff chipmunk, white-throated swift, and tree lizard are also found here. Mountain lions, almost never seen, dwell in these rugged areas.

The shrublands house a wonderful array of creatures, from the Ord's kangaroo rat and loggerhead shrike to the sage thrasher, sage grouse, Brewer's sparrow, desert cottontail rabbit, black-tailed jackrabbit, short-horned and sagebrush lizards, short-eared owl, spotted and green-tailed towhees, black-throated sparrow, and western scrub jay.

ACTIVITIES

■ **CAMPING:** Primitive camping is permitted year-round on the refuge's west side at Swinging Bridge Campground and on the refuge's east end at Crook Campground. Both are located close to the auto-tour route and have wheelchair-accessible restrooms. Crook features accessible grills but no other facilities. No reservations and no fees.

■ **WILDLIFE OBSERVATION:** Due to the refuge's remote location and the fact that wildlife is active primarily at dawn and dusk, visitors interested in getting the best experience from Browns should consider camping, either on-site or on other public lands nearby—of which there are plenty. Spring and fall here offer the richest samplings of wildlife, not to mention the greatest comfort level for visitors. Spring songbird migration is at its busiest between late May and late June; fall migrants appear from late August through mid-September. Wildlife activity is scant by comparison in July and August. Intrepid types will have a superb visit in winter, with great herds of mule deer, elk, and bald eagles along the river. Access is good throughout the year with the exception of early spring—usually April—when roads turn to slop.

BROWNS PARK HUNTING AND FISHING SEASONS

Hunting
(Seasons may vary)

	Jan	Feb	Mar	Apr	May	Jun	Jul	Aug	Sep	Oct	Nov	Dec
antelope, elk, and mule deer (using following hunting methods)												
bow								■	■			
muzzle-loader									■			
firearm										■	■	
geese	■										■	■
ducks	■									■	■	■

Fishing

	Jan	Feb	Mar	Apr	May	Jun	Jul	Aug	Sep	Oct	Nov	Dec
carp	■	■	■	■	■	■	■	■	■	■	■	■
catfish	■	■	■	■	■	■	■	■	■	■	■	■
trout	■	■	■	■	■	■	■	■	■	■	■	■

Big game (**antelope, elk**, and **mule deer**) bow-hunting season runs from late Aug. to late Sept.; muzzle-loader season runs for a week in mid-Sept.; and rifle season is during Oct. and early Nov. For more information on the current hunting and fishing regulations for Browns Park NWR, including license requirements, seasons, and bag limits, consult refuge office.

■ **PHOTOGRAPHY:** Sage grouse hold their annual, spectacular courtship displays on two leks in mid to late March; because there are no blinds on-site, you may need to bring portable blinds to get a good shot. Wildflowers and desert shrubs such as rabbit brush and spiny hopsage bloom in late spring and early summer, as do cacti. Browns Park is an excellent place to photograph mule deer; does with yearlings arrive the first few days of November to spend the winter; bucks, in full regalia, arrive two or so weeks later and remain on site until January.

■ **HIKES AND WALKS:** Browns Park is highly accessible to foot travel, with a network of unimproved refuge roads accessing all major areas and one nature foot trail, but no developed long-distance hiking trails. The Vermillion Creek area at the refuge's south end is a beautiful spot to explore, with cottonwood forests and sandbars on the Green River, and grasslands, shrublands, and piñon-juniper forests in close proximity.

■ **PUBLICATIONS:** Refuge brochure with map; bird checklist.

Rocky Mountain Arsenal NWR
Commerce City, Colorado

Mule deer bucks sparring, Rocky Mountain Arsenal NWR

If the vision of Rocky Mountain Arsenal refuge (RMA) is realized—if these 27 square miles of prairie, woodlands, and ponds that once adjoined a chemical weapons facility are restored to their natural splendor and productivity—then most anything is possible. And the vision is progressing, well ahead of schedule. The arsenal, like a few other new-era refuges, is not so much about preservation as restoration: re-creating a long-lost native landscape. It's a Herculean effort, rife with lessons, and perhaps a blueprint for other regions of postindustrial America.

President Theodore Roosevelt was prescient in saying "...nothing short of defending this country in wartime compares in importance with the great central task of leaving this land even a better land for our descendants than it is for us." Today, looking out over this sprawling refuge, the conservationist president himself would be stunned by the special meaning his words have for this former munitions facility, now being restored as an urban wildlife refuge.

HISTORY

Fast forward through Arapaho and Cheyenne cultures, bison on shortgrass prairie, homesteaders of the mid-1800s. Stop at 1982. The Rocky Mountain Arsenal ceases production. Over the previous 40 years, deadly chemical inventions—mustard gas, white phosphorous, and napalm for use in World War II and Korea, and later a variety of pesticides—were manufactured here, first by the U.S. Army, and later by Shell Oil Company. Groundwater contamination from toxic byproducts first appeared in the 1950s. Cleanup efforts, including plans for treating groundwater, were inching ahead by 1974. In 1987 the Arsenal was named a federal Superfund site.

Outdoor classroom, Rocky Mountain Arsenal NWR

Throughout it all, endangered bald eagles arrived each year to winter in a secluded woodland roost on Arsenal grounds. The U.S. Fish & Wildlife Service discovered the roost in 1986 and in short order documented some 300 other species using the woodlands, lakes, and prairie. In a strange twist of fate, the Arsenal, a place nobody really cared to visit, had been functioning as a wildlife haven in the middle of Denver. F&W served initially as an overseer of wildlife while containment and cleanup work began; then, public interest in the natural values of the Arsenal spurred a major campaign to designate the area a sanctuary. The goal was realized in 1992, with passage of the Rocky Mountain Arsenal NWR Act by Congress.

Much work remains to be done. Cleanup projects, costing some $2.2 billion, are scheduled to be completed by 2011, although these efforts, are at this time well ahead of schedule. Public use of the area will be carefully controlled until all projects are complete. A highly impressive plan for the refuge *after* cleanup—including habitat restoration, visitor trams, outdoor classrooms, a science and technology center—is taking shape, with strong community support. If financial support continues, the Arsenal in years to come may take its rightful place as one of the nation's great urban wildlife refuges.

GETTING THERE

RMA refuge is located 10 mi. northeast of downtown Denver; the main entrance, from which visitors can take a shuttle to the Visitor Center, is accessed via 72nd Ave. and Quebec. The Eagle Watch area on the refuge's eastern boundary is located on Buckley Rd., between 56th and 96th avenues.

■ **SEASON:** Open year-round.

■ **HOURS:** Daylight hours; Visitor Center, with outstanding interpretive exhibits on the Arsenal's natural and social history, is open Saturdays, 8 a.m.–3 p.m.

■ **FEES:** None.

■ **ADDRESS:** Building 111, Commerce City, CO 80022-1748

■ **TELEPHONE:** 303/298-0232 for prerecorded message with visitation options.

TOURING THE ARSENAL

Public access to the refuge is restricted at this time as cleanup efforts continue. Scheduled trolley tours allow visitors to view all major habitats, see wildlife, and view remediation projects from a distance. Between 11,000 and 12,000 people per year are now visiting the refuge.

■ **BY AUTOMOBILE:** No auto touring.

■ **BY BUS:** Prearranged bus tours, depart from the refuge's west gate and allow visitors to see all major habitats and witness the remediation process.

■ **BY FOOT:** Limited areas are open to foot travel at this time. There are guided walks through prairie, wetland, and woodland areas. Generally, hiking here is not permitted.

■ **BY BICYCLE:** Scheduled "bike the refuge" programs are offered throughout the year.

■ **BY CANOE, KAYAK, OR BOAT:** Not permitted.

WHAT TO SEE

■ **LANDSCAPE AND CLIMATE** This gently rolling, open terrain would almost certainly be prime urban real estate by now had it not been for the lethal items developed in two clusters of buildings known as the North and South plants. Even in the 1940s, when technology governing the production and disposal of hazardous materials was in its infancy, the U.S. military for safety and security reasons maintained a 14,000-acre buffer zone around production sites. These outlying lands, including a series of lakes originally built for irrigation of croplands, were subject to far lesser degrees of contamination than other areas, and they maintained a remarkable array of wildlife throughout the years of weapons and pesticide production.

The core areas, comprising about one-third of the site, were another matter. In what was considered a secure disposal method at the time, chemicals from production areas were often sluiced into big earthen pits lined with asphalt. These liners later settled, buckled, and cracked, sending unwanted chemicals into groundwater and soils. The buildings themselves, like giant sponges, collected all manner of agents. Wildlife mortalities, most notably birds, were associated with core areas as recently as 1996.

Remediation efforts, however, are revamping the landscape once again. A water treatment system cleanses

American kestrel

more than one billion gallons of groundwater annually, meeting state and federal clean-water guidelines before water flows off-site. Great volumes of soil have been removed to landfills or capped and covered with fresh topsoil. The resulting mounds, planted with native grasses, bear witness to days past, as do the ancient tipi rings found in other areas here.

Elevation at RMA averages 5,300 feet. Winters are moderately cold, with snow often melting soon after it falls. Spring, summer, and fall are mild, with most precipitation occurring in May and June.

■ PLANT LIFE AND HABITATS

Prairie Shortgrass prairie once dominated Arsenal lands, a mixture of such grasses as western wheatgrass, buffalo grass, and needle-and-thread, with scatterings of plains prickly pear and hedgehog cactus, yucca, rabbitbrush, and many wildflowers—asters, plains coreopsis, primroses, and skeletonweed, among others. In drier, sandy soils was a sandhills prairie community; sand bluestem and prairie sandreed were important grasses, along with sand sage; native forbs such as bush morning glory, several goldenrod species, and native sunflowers bloomed seasonally.

Settlement and farming here altered much of the prairie landscape long before the days of chemical production: Many areas were plowed for croplands, others converted to "tame" grasses such as bromes and bluegrass. Crested wheatgrass, a non-native variety with minimal value to wildlife, was planted to mitigate soil erosion. Later Alfalfa, sweet clover, and other exotic species such as cheatgrass, Canada thistle, and Russian knapweed arrived on the scene.

A sizable amount of prairie remains today relatively intact; yet other areas are degraded, as much from nonnative species as chemical contaminants. Cleanup work under way presents an opportunity for prairie restoration. The refuge has as its goal the restoration of 8,000 acres to native grasslands. It's a slow, labor-intensive process, one far more complicated than merely tossing seeds into the

Black-tailed prairie dog

wind. Once restored, the new prairie will need fire and grazing to keep it healthy; the American bison, that hulking, somber grassland steward of old, may be brought in to resume its duties. (See also the National Bison Range refuge.)

Woodlands Some trees may have grown here prior to settlement—which species and where they grew is all but impossible to know. What's growing today are plains cottonwoods, white poplar, New Mexico locust, some Siberian elm, Russian olive, several nonnative conifer species, and such native shrubs as hackberry and western snowberry. Woodlands occur primarily along First Creek and the Lakes area and provide very good habitat for a variety of songbirds and, on the creek, for bald eagles. Future restoration of woodlands will rely heavily upon three native species—plains cottonwood, peachleaf willow, and hackberry.

Wetlands On the margins of the lakes, and in a new wetland area planned on the southeast corner of the refuge, belts of cattail and bulrush envelope shallower inlets and canals, along with some amount of wet meadow communities—including many species of sedges and rushes. Submergent plants such as smartweed and milfoil occur in the lakes, providing food for waterfowl.

■ ANIMAL LIFE

Birds Never far from prairie dog colonies are burrowing owls, another fascinating prairie species seen frequently here spring through fall. Dusky brown, with vivid yellow eyes, they stand about 10 inches high on long, skinny legs. Active in daylight, they seldom wander far from the safety of their dens, which they appropriate from prairie dogs and other burrowing animals and line with manure.

For sheer visual splendor, the American bald eagle is tough to beat. Each winter they return to the Arsenal in numbers ranging from 10 to 80 or more, commandeering the mature cottonwood trees along First Creek. While fish—dead, dying or otherwise vulnerable—are the usual draw for bald eagles, the big birds here spend most of their time hunting prairie dogs and other rodents.

Mammals Living proof of the Arsenal's grassland vitality is its abundant population of black-tailed prairie dogs. One of the most commonly seen mammals here, these sociable little squirrels are a focal point of native prairie biomes. Their subterranean living quarters, complete with a separate "toilet" chamber, lie some 14 feet beneath the surface; on top, they maintain small domes of dirt near entrance holes, ideal vantage points from which to scan for danger. They eat primarily grasses; their burrowing and grazing activities aerate the soil and help to keep grasslands vigorous. Unlike many prairie rodents, black-tailed prairie dogs remain active during all but the coldest days of winter.

Both mule deer, a Rocky Mountain native, and white-tailed deer, a relative newcomer, are common on the refuge, challenging visitors to hone their deer identification skills. The "mulie" has larger ears and a black-tipped tail; the "white-tail," true to its name, has an oversized tail colored vivid white on the underside. When alarmed, the latter species raises its tail like a flag, bounding off.

ACTIVITIES

■ **CAMPING AND SWIMMING:** Not permitted.

■ **WILDLIFE OBSERVATION:** The Eagle Watch Viewing Area on Buckley Road on the refuge's east side is a premier locale for observing bald eagles, from Feburary through April. American white pelicans are a glorious sight in summer.

■ **PHOTOGRAPHY:** Photo tours are led by refuge staff; contact refuge for details.

> **HUNTING AND FISHING**
> Fishing is permitted seasonally on Arsenal lakes; restrictions apply; contact refuge for details. Hunting is not permitted on refuge land.

■ **SEASONAL EVENTS:** January: Eagle Fest; April: Earth Day celebration; October: National Wildlife Refuge Week.

■ **PUBLICATIONS:** Bird, mammal, and reptile/amphibian checklists; a visitor guide, "Discover a New Refuge," with overview of refuge plans; publications and updates on remediation projects.

Bear Lake NWR
Southeast Idaho Refuge Complex, Webster, Idaho

Willet in marsh

Best known for its extensive wetlands preserving historic Dingle Swamp, 19,000-acre Bear Lake NWR contains a unique landscape of southeastern Idaho: a sprawling marsh-and-lake complex in an otherwise high-elevation valley.

HISTORY

Bear Lake NWR was established in 1968 to provide habitat for Canada geese, sandhill cranes, redhead duck, and other migratory birds. Since then, canvasback duck and white-faced ibis have declined elsewhere, and refuge management now makes these species a priority. Trumpeter swans, inhabitants of the area 100 years ago, are returning on their spring and fall migrations.

GETTING THERE

From Montpelier, travel west on US 89 for 3 mi., turning left at Bear Lake County Airport Rd. Continue 5 mi. to refuge entrance road.
- **SEASON:** Open year-round.
- **HOURS:** Daylight hours, refuge office hours, 8 a.m.–4:30 p.m., Mon.–Fri.
- **FEES:** None.
- **ADDRESS:** Refuge headquarters at 370 Webster St., Montpelier ID 83254
- **TELEPHONE:** 208/847-1757

TOURING BEAR LAKE

- **BY AUTOMOBILE:** Salt Meadow Wildlife Observation Route is open year-round, but there are periods of deep snow, which may restrict travel in the winter months (closed September 25–January 15). County roads encircling the refuge are open year-round.
- **BY FOOT:** All refuge roads are open to foot travel; other areas are available for exploration July 1–February 29, except those seasonally closed. Foot travel

along the south dike of Salt Meadow Unit is permitted September 25–January 15. Foot travel is allowed at that time on the Rainbow Dike, however. Cross-country skiing is also allowed in these areas.

■ **BY BICYCLE:** Bicycles are welcome on graveled roads year-round, but not on trails.

■ **BY CANOE, KAYAK, OR BOAT:** Motorized and nonmotorized boats may be used in designated areas, September 25–January 15. North Beach State Park, on the southern boundary of the refuge, offers boat-launching facilities.

WHAT TO SEE

■ **LANDSCAPE AND CLIMATE** The mountain-ringed Bear Valley lies at 5,925 feet; elevations range up to 6,800 feet on the slopes of Merkley Mountain. The refuge's stream-fed marshlands form the northern end of Bear Lake. Summer temperatures at these elevations seldom top 90 degrees Fahrenheit; just 10 to 12 inches of precipitation fall annually.

■ **PLANT LIFE AND HABITATS**
Open water and wetlands The refuge preserves much of the historic Dingle Swamp, a mosaic of bulrush and cattail marsh, mudflats, wet meadows of sedges, rushes, and grasses, and smaller satellite lakes, ponds, and marshes. Water from the Bear River is diverted into the marsh complex through a canal and flows south out of the refuge into Bear Lake. Several slow-moving creeks, including Bloomington, Spring, and Paris, enter the marsh along the refuge's western boundary, passing through stands of willows and wet meadows as they enter the refuge marsh.
Grasslands A small portion of refuge holdings include native grasslands of salt grass, wild rye, and western wheatgrass.
Arid lands Along the base of Merkley Mountain are semi-arid shrublands of sagebrush, rabbitbrush, and greasewood, with an understory of native grasses, including wheatgrass.

■ **ANIMAL LIFE** The size and diversity of marshlands and open waters provide an increasingly rare commodity for wildlife—isolation. The marsh features almost impenetrable stands of bulrush, or "tules," used by many water-associated birds for nesting sites.

Bear Lake houses one of North America's largest nesting populations of white-faced ibis, the marquee attraction of the refuge. Watch for their cup-shaped nesting platforms amid the bulrushes in summer. Caspian, Forster's, and black terns nest in the marsh as well, along with such waterfowl as redhead ducks, ruddy ducks, and cinnamon teal. Nesting shorebirds include the American avocet and black-necked stilt, willet, and northern phalarope; look for the glorious American white pelican in summer and fall. A sharp-eyed observer might spot a trumpeter swan

Wilson's phalarope

out on the refuge ponds. The shrublands and adjacent mountain slopes support thriving populations of elk, mule deer, and moose.

ACTIVITIES

■ **CAMPING:** No camping is permitted on the refuge.

■ **SWIMMING:** North Beach State Park, on the southern end of the refuge, is open to swimming; no swimming is permitted on Bear Lake refuge.

■ **WILDLIFE OBSERVATION:** Spring, summer, and fall occur in rapid succession in this high mountain valley; waterfowl arrive in March, ibis, terns, and grebes in late April to mid-May; by June the place is jumping, with goslings and ducklings on parade. By August, most shorebirds and songbirds depart. Winter visitors to the refuge will observe large herds of mule deer along Merkley Mountain and maybe even an occasional bald eagle.

■ **PHOTOGRAPHY:** The Salt Meadow Wildlife Route provides some of the best access to marshland species and scenery. Boat trips present photo opportunities of the refuge's bird population; boating is allowed after September 24.

HUNTING AND FISHING
Bear Lake to the south has an excellent fishery, but marsh waters are unproductive. Waterfowl and upland-game hunting opportunities are provided on the refuge.

■ **HIKES AND WALKS:** You can explore marshlands, wet meadows, and open waters via unimproved roads (locally also called trails) at the end of the Salt Meadow Route and off Paris-Dingle Road. Though marshy and muddy, a cross-country hike south from the Salt Meadow Route to Bunn Lake offers fine viewing of refuge birdlife. Parking and walking around Merkley Lake on the east side of the refuge.

■ **SEASONAL EVENTS:** None.

■ **PUBLICATIONS:** Bird checklist; map with touring and habitat information; general refuge leaflet, with map.

Camas NWR
Southeast Idaho Refuge Complex, Hamer, Idaho

Trumpeter swans

An oasis amid fields of potatoes and alfalfa, 10,578-acre Camas NWR preserves marshlands and wet meadows in this corner of the Snake River Plain. Undeveloped but accessible, this refuge hosts a wealth of nesting shorebirds and other water-dependent species. For now, visitation numbers are low, which means that the lucky few who come to see this, the former hunting grounds of the Blackfeet tribe, have no crowds to contend with.

HISTORY

Much of Camas remains unchanged from its days as the Blackfeet hunting range. Rat Farm Pond is all that survives from a muskrat-rearing enterprise that came and went prior to establishment of the refuge in 1937. Camas in 1977 was combined with the Minidoka, Bear Lake, and Grays Lake refuges as the Southeast Idaho Refuge Complex, with headquarters in Pocatello. Peregrine falcons were reintroduced here in 1983.

GETTING THERE

From the town of Hamer, located 35 mi. north of Idaho Falls on I-15, travel north out of town along Frontage Rd. for 3 mi., turning left at the refuge sign onto access road; continue 2 mi. to refuge headquarters.

■ **SEASON:** Open year-round.

■ **HOURS:** Open a half-hour before sunrise to a half-hour after sunset. Refuge headquarters open weekdays, intermittently, 8 a.m.–4:30 p.m.

■ **FEES:** None.

■ **ADDRESS:** 2150 E. 2350 North, Hamer, ID 83425

■ **TELEPHONE:** 208/662-5423

TOURING CAMAS

■ **BY AUTOMOBILE:** A great number of gravel refuge roads are here, following Camas Creek and traversing all major habitats, including marshes and lakes, both large and small.

■ **BY FOOT:** Excellent hiking opportunities exist along all gravel refuge roads year-round; hiking off-road is permitted anywhere between July 16 and March 31. Cross-coutnry skiing and snowshoeing are allowed on roads and off-road during the same period.

■ **BY BICYCLE:** Biking is permitted on roads open to vehicular travel.

■ **BY CANOE, KAYAK, OR BOAT:** No boating is permitted at Camas.

WHAT TO SEE

■ **LANDSCAPE AND CLIMATE** Camas lies on the northeastern edge of the Snake River Plain, a vast, semiarid landscape of rolling hills covering the southern third of Idaho. Much of the plain has been converted to agriculture. At an elevation of 4,800 feet, the climate here is typical of the intermountain region: dry, mild summers and cold winters. Average precipitation totals less than 9 inches.

Long-billed curlew

■ **PLANT LIFE AND HABITATS**
Wetlands The availability and quality of water are important at Camas, 60 percent of which consists of wetlands. Camas Creek is the primary water source for these productive marshes, wet meadows, and saline semiwet meadows, with plant life ranging from hardstem bulrush to inland salt grass and Nebraska sedge. Fed by snowmelt from adjacent mountains, the creek dwindles by midsummer, and then the refuge depends on nine wells to keep wetlands going. Steady use of groundwater by agriculture and food-processing plants has lowered the water table.

Arid lands Bounding the complex of "wet" are some 3,633 acres of "dry," a sagebrush steppe dominated by basin big sagebrush, along with Wyoming big sagebrush, antelope bitterbrush, rabbit brushes, and some fourwing saltbush.

Dominant grasses include needle-and-thread and Indian ricegrass, which in large stands presents a golden-yellow wash of color. A modest display of wildflowers is also present—showy milkweed, among them. Milkweed has pink flowers and produces a large, swollen pod from which dandelion-like seedheads are released. Evening primrose, with night-blooming white flowers, blooms in early to midsummer.

■ **ANIMAL LIFE** A superb array of wetland-associated birds is here: Black-necked stilt, sandhill crane, long-billed curlew, snowy egret, American avocet, and Wilson's phalarope all nest on-site. Less common nesting species at Camus include the trumpeter swan and white-faced ibis. Some 15 species of duck nest here as well. In summer four tern species—Caspian, common, Forster's, and black—are present, along with American white pelicans and the semipalmated plover. Camas is frequented by moose, readily encountered in the willow thickets along Camas Creek. Other water-associated mammals include beaver, muskrat, and a recent arrival—the raccoon, first confirmed here in 1995.

Raptors are well represented; the golden eagle, prairie and peregrine falcon, Swainson's hawk, northern goshawk, red-tailed hawk, and ferruginous hawk may be spotted, often on the prowl in the air, year-round. Pronghorn, mule deer, white-tailed jackrabbit, and coyote frequent the uplands; birds such as the sage grouse, sage thrasher, black-billed magpie, and horned lark are seen in these higher areas as well.

ACTIVITIES

■ **CAMPING:** No camping is permitted on the refuge; camping facilities are available at Stoddard Creek Campground and at a county park near the town of Roberts, both 20 miles away; camping is also available on national forest lands 40 miles north.

■ **WILDLIFE OBSERVATION:** Come to see birds at Camas, especially marsh-associated birds, mid-May through July, when they are most abundant. Your chances of spotting moose, pronghorn, and other mammals are pretty even, year-round. Fall and winter are the better times in this region to look for raptors, including bald eagles.

■ **PHOTOGRAPHY:** Camas makes a good site for photographing sandhill cranes, herons, and shorebirds. If it's flowers you like to photograph, the surrounding steppe desert's blooming shrubs and wildflowers are gorgeous in June.

■ **HIKES AND WALKS:** Serious birders have discovered the Camas warbler and songbird migration, and there's a popular walk through cottonwoods and box elders along the banks of Camas Creek. The footpath begins near refuge headquarters; it's possible to walk for a half-mile or more. Mid-May to mid-June and mid-August to mid-September are prime periods. May and June are excellent times to glimpse both common and rare warblers and other small songbirds as they stop over to feed in the groves of trees around the headquarters building.

■ **SEASONAL EVENTS:** None.

■ **PUBLICATIONS:** Refuge brochure, bird checklist.

Deer Flat NWR
Nampa, Idaho

Golden eagle

The manufactured western oasis has a singular appearance: The water seems flatter than flat, and there's lots of it. It's fringed by verdant margins of implanted deciduous trees—tangled willow, cottonwood, Russian olive—bearing familiar shades of green. There are ample "recreation areas"—meaning access points for power boats and water skiing—and the whole works is situated within a parched landscape, the natural landscape of sagebrush, sun-scorched flats, and rolling hills, a world with little use for water.

The often generic qualities of such places belie their value for wildlife, and 11,430-acre Deer Flat NWR is a perfect example. On the western side of Idaho, on the inner edge of the Pacific Flyway, Deer Flat offers just what shorebirds, waterfowl, warblers—even owls—are looking for. Birds are the primary attraction here, and diversity is high year-round—tremendous, even, during migration. Another draw is the Snake River. Along a 113-mile corridor stretching west into Oregon, visitors with the right watercraft can explore numerous islands that are home to a great array of native species.

HISTORY

Like so many regions of the West, the story of Deer Flat is one of bringing water to the desert. Some water was here; in the area that is today the refuge, a low swale with springs grew an abundance of grass. Elk and mule deer, fleeing harsh winters in nearby mountains, gathered in this area to feed, giving this place its name.

When President Theodore Roosevelt created the Bureau of Reclamation (BOR) in 1902, Boise landowners recognized an opportunity to convert sagebrush to cash crops. A man named J. H. Lowell was instrumental in securing a commitment from the BOR for a large-scale irrigation project. Between 1906 and 1909, a $2.5-million project ensued, with a reservoir constructed and the "New York Canal"—named for the hometown of the investors—installed on the Boise

River to divert water into the new pools. The result, a 9,000-acre lake, supplied water to irrigate 200,000 acres of croplands.

Roosevelt declared Deer Flat a wildlife refuge in 1909, though it remained unstaffed until 1937, when the Snake River Migratory Waterfowl Refuge was created. Each remained a separate refuge until they were merged in 1963. About 90,000 people visit Deer Flat each year.

GETTING THERE

Deer Flat is located in Nampa, ID, about 15 mi. west of Boise on I-84. From downtown Nampa, drive south on 12th St. to Lake Lowell Ave.; turn right and continue west 4 mi. to the refuge headquarters.

■ **SEASON:** Open year-round.

■ **HOURS:** Open daylight hours; refuge headquarters and Visitor Center, with interpretive exhibits and displays, are open weekdays, 7:30 a.m.–4 p.m.

■ **FEES:** None.

■ **ADDRESS:** 13751 Upper Embankment Rd., Nampa, ID 83686

■ **TELEPHONE:** 208/467-9278

TOURING DEER FLAT

■ **BY AUTOMOBILE:** The refuge offers excellent access for wildlife observation. A 29.5-mile refuge auto birding tour (the accompanying brochure is extremely useful) begins at the east end of Upper Dam. A driving tour (and accompanying brochure) of the Snake River is also available.

■ **BY FOOT:** Most foot travel takes place along 10 miles of refuge roads encircling Lake Lowell. The 0.75-mi. Headquarters Trail is self-guided. Foot access to islands in the Snake River Sector is prohibited between February 1 and May 31 to protect migratory birds. Cross-country skiing and ice skating are permitted in all recreation areas as conditions allow.

■ **BY BICYCLE:** The refuge offers lots of potential biking opportunities. Biking is permitted year-round in all developed recreation areas and along refuge roads and maintained trails. The south side of Lake Lowell is flat; the north side features some sizable hills. The terrain is generally wide open, offering expansive views.

■ **BY CANOE, KAYAK, OR BOAT:** Lake Lowell is open to power boats and sailboats between April 15 and September 30. Water skiing, jet skiing, and sailboarding are very popular; the lake is not much of an opportunity for paddlers. The Snake River Sector, consisting of 113 river miles, with numerous islands used by nesting waterfowl and other wildlife, is accessible only by boat. Check at the Visitor Center for current conditions and launching sites on the river.

WHAT TO SEE

■ **LANDSCAPE AND CLIMATE** Deer Flat is located in southwestern Idaho, in the Boise Valley about 15 miles east of the Oregon state line. The refuge and valley are part of the Snake River Plain, a semiarid to arid region of rolling hills, through which the powerful Snake River has carved a series of deep, often spectacular canyons. Prior to settlement, this region featured unbroken expanses of sagebrush steppe, stretching east to the Boise Front, where Idaho's share of the Rocky Mountains rises abruptly from the plain, and to the southwest, into the desolate slopes and canyons of the Owyhee Mountains. The refuge lies at an elevation of about 2,500 feet.

The climate here features dry, cloudless summers, with high temperatures in the 90s. Compared with the adjacent mountains, winters are cool and mild, and

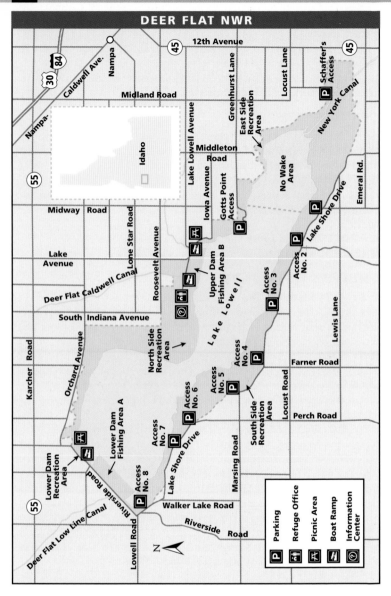

DEER FLAT NWR

most snow that falls doesn't stick around long. Most precipitation accumulates during the winter or in spring, but all told the area receives a scant 11 inches (average) annually.

The dominant feature of the refuge is Lake Lowell, one of the largest "off-river" impoundments in the West; without the Boise River to replenish it, however, it would not exit. Maximum lake depth is about 45 feet, though in most areas it is closer to 20 feet. This warm-water fishery is popular with anglers.

Deer Flat's other refuge unit is the Snake River Sector, a reasonably good place to see this powerful western river as it emerges from canyons to the east and flows across open plains. Beginning at the Canyon/Ada county line, the refuge corridor extends 113 miles to Farewell Bend, in Oregon. Some 94 islands (there are many more) are within refuge boundaries, ranging in size from 1 to 58 acres.

■ PLANT LIFE AND HABITATS

Wetlands The Boise Valley has always been an important wintering area for waterfowl on the Pacific Flyway; the creation of Lake Lowell added a substantial piece of habitat for their needs. The lake fills with spring snowmelt, then diminishes through the summer as water is utilized for irrigation. This yearly "draw down" creates expansive shallows where aquatic vegetation, especially smartweed, grows in abundance. Mudflats, too, are created, supporting a rich array of invertebrate life that attracts shorebirds.

Arid lands A small portion of Deer Flat includes uplands of native sagebrush steppe, with greasewood, big sagebrush, and rabbit brush varieties; grasses include Great Basin wild rye and exotic species, including cheatgrass, an introduced grass that regrows quickly after a fire. A similar plant community exists on many of the islands in the Snake River Sector.

Forests Thickets of riparian woodlands—primarily willows, mature stands of cottonwood, and Russian olive—occupy exposed fingers of land and shoreline surrounding Lake Lowell; the north side of the lake features the heaviest concentrations. Many of the islands in the lower portion of the Snake River Sector feature tangled woodlands of willow, box elder, maple, and cottonwood.

■ ANIMAL LIFE

Birds Birding is special at Deer Flat, particularly during spring and fall migration, and refuge staff have a wealth of information on where and when many uncommon species show up. The highlights that follow focus primarily on the unusual or notable migrants; many other birds are readily seen year-round.

When the mudflats appear on Lake Lowell, shorebirds materialize. White-faced ibis, American golden plover, stilt sandpiper, short-billed

Short-eared owl

dowitcher, and the parasitic jaeger (a gull-like bird) have all been seen. The Pacific loon, Bonaparte's and Sabine's gulls, along with bald eagles, pass through.

Owls are diverse: The burrowing, long-eared, short-eared, northern saw-whet, western screech, barn, and great horned all nest on-site, though are more readily spotted in winter. The northern pygmy owl is sighted rarely, as is the snowy owl in winter. You have a good chance of seeing and hearing several song-bird species during migration. They include a wealth of warblers—the Nashville, palm, and Townsend's, among many others—along with white-throated sparrow, least flycatcher, evening grosbeak, Vaux's swift, and Say's phoebe. Raptors cruising high in the skies during migration include northern goshawk, golden eagle, gyrfalcon (an Arctic falcon that is the largest of the falcons), and Cooper's hawk.

Mammals Though birds are by far the primary attraction here, a number of mammals are present, and a few notable species may be seen in areas that receive less recreational use or during periods of the day and year when things are quiet.

This is kangaroo rat country, and Deer Flat supports a thriving population of the Ord's kangaroo rat. Look in upland areas for burrow entrances, about 3 inches in diameter, on slopes and around shrubs. A tap at the entrance just might trigger a drumming from inside, as the Ord's thumps its large hind feet to signal danger. When sitting or moving slowly, its lengthy tail leaves a very clear drag mark on the ground.

Another readily seen mammal is the mule deer, present year-round. The Nuttall's cottontail, red fox, coyote, beaver, muskrat and mink are abundant. Less often seen are the pygmy rabbit, raccoon, white-tailed jackrabbit, and badger. River otters (deep brown on top, shiny silver below) are present year-round but less easy to encounter. You might look for their slides worn into riverbanks.

Reptiles and amphibians The gopher snake and garter snake are common and may be seen spring through fall; also present is one species of horned lizard.

Fish Lake Lowell supports a fishery of largemouth and smallmouth bass, bluegill, catfish, crappie and yellow perch.

Ord's kangaroo rat

ACTIVITIES

■ **CAMPING:** Camping is not permitted on the refuge; camping is available at Eagle Island and Veterans Memorial state parks, east and north of the refuge along ID 55.

■ **SWIMMING:** Swimming is permitted in designated areas at Upper and Lower Embankments in Lake Lowell. Swimming is not permited in the canal.

■ **WILDLIFE OBSERVATION:** April and May are prime months for the spring songbird migration at Deer Flat, and a good time to see many other species as well. Access to much of the refuge is closed between October 1 and April 14, but areas around refuge headquarters are very productive, and refuge staff will gladly suggest other places to try.

■ **PHOTOGRAPHY:** There are fine opportunities to photograph vast flocks of waterfowl and concentrations of shorebirds around Lake Lowell. During quiet times, upland wildlife such as mule deer and small mammals may be captured on film. Photographers with the appropriate boat will find the Snake River Sector outstanding for landscape images; islands offer other great opportunities.

■ **HIKES AND WALKS:** Drive to the Teal Lane parking area to Headquarters Trail, and take a very pleasant stroll through some of Deer Flat's most extensive mature woodlands—enough to qualify as "timber." This is a prime area for songbirds and owls.

■ **SEASONAL EVENTS:** The refuge celebrated its 90th birthday on October 16, 1999, with tours, displays, and featured speakers. Call the refuge for information on future seasonal events.

■ **PUBLICATIONS:** Refuge brochure; checklists of birds and mammals; maps of refuge units.

HUNTING AND FISHING
Hunting is permitted for **upland birds** during Sept.; **ducks** and **coot** from Oct. through mid-Jan.; and **mule deer** Oct. to Nov.

Fishing is permitted year-round on Lake Lowell and Snake River Island Sector. Anglers catch **largemouth bass, bullhead, crappie, trout, perch, bluegill, smallmouth bass**, and **channel catfish**.

Grays Lake NWR
Southeast Idaho Refuge Complex, Wayan, Idaho

Green-winged teal

John Grey might be disoriented by the tourist sights of present-day Jackson, Wyoming, across the state line, but this 19th-century mountain man would almost surely recognize the lake and refuge that today bear his name—if in fact he was ever really here. So it goes with names and places. The lake is Grays Lake, and the refuge—a remote valley rimmed with open hills and long-backed mountains cloaked in aspen and conifers—ensures that these 18,300 acres remain wild and largely undisturbed. Visitors to the refuge share this magnificent space with only about 1,200 people per year.

HISTORY

It has never been confirmed that John Grey, a member of an 1818 trapping expedition in this country, actually set eyes upon the lake. Grey and his contemporaries did trade with the northern Shoshoni Indians, a wealthy, hospitable people whose lands encompassed the Grand Tetons and Wind River Mountains to the northeast. Between 1860 and the turn of the century, settlers passed along the southern boundary of the refuge following the Lander Cut-off of the Oregon Trail. In 1906 a massive water diversion effort known as Clark's Cut was initiated here, much to the detriment of wetlands. Still operational today, this canal may be seen along Highway 34 at the lake's southwestern edge.

Established in 1965, the refuge in 1978 became the test site for an important experiment to save the endangered whooping crane. Eggs from whooping cranes were placed in nests of sandhill cranes here; it was believed the sandhills would rear the whoopers as their own, teaching them migratory routes and survival skills. By 1985, some 33 whooping cranes were fledged, many of them summering at Grays Lake with foster parents and kin. Ultimately, the experiment proved unsuccessful. Raised by sandhill cranes, the whoopers failed to pair off with their own kind and never reproduced. In the absence of breeding, the Grays Lake flock of whooping cranes has steadily diminished, leaving perhaps three individuals surviving today.

GETTING THERE

From Soda Springs, ID, travel north on ID 34 for 33 mi., turning north at refuge sign onto a gravel road; refuge headquarters is located 3 mi. ahead.

From Jackson, WY, travel south on US 191 for 14 mi., bearing right onto US 89; continue south on US 89 for 36 mi., turning right (west) onto ID 34 at the town of Freedom, WY; continue 20 mi. through the town of Wayan to the refuge.

- **SEASON:** Open year-round.
- **HOURS:** Daylight hours; refuge headquarters, with interpretive exhibits and displays, is open daily, 7 a.m.–4:30 p.m. from April 1 through November 15.
- **FEES:** None.
- **ADDRESS:** 74 Grays Lake Rd., Wayan, ID 83285
- **TELEPHONE:** 208/574-2755

TOURING GRAYS LAKE

- **BY AUTOMOBILE:** Visitors may tour on gravel and unimproved roads year-round, unless posted otherwise; landowner permission is required to enter some refuge areas—be sure to leave gates as they stand, open or closed. Refuge roads are daunting to traverse in early spring and impassable in winter. Snow is possible in early fall.
- **BY FOOT:** Hiking is permitted in the northern half of the refuge between September 20 and March 31; permission from private landowners is necessary to enter some refuge lands.

Peregrine falcon

- **BY BICYCLE:** No biking is permitted on the refuge.
- **BY CANOE, KAYAK, OR BOAT:** Motors are not permitted, and the potential for boating is limited by shallow depths and vegetation; the north end may be the best bet for boating.

WHAT TO SEE

- **LANDSCAPE AND CLIMATE** Located just 56 miles southwest of Grand Teton National Park, Grays Lake is on the periphery of a vast, largely intact core of wild lands known as the Greater Yellowstone Ecosystem. Immediately east are massive upthrusts—the Salt River and Gros Ventre ranges of the Rockies; immediately west is the sprawling Snake River Plain. The same fiery mantle plume, or hotspot, that burned through the earth's crust to inundate the plain repeatedly with lava is today centered beneath Yellowstone National Park to the north, powering its geysers and mudpots.

GRAYS LAKE NWR

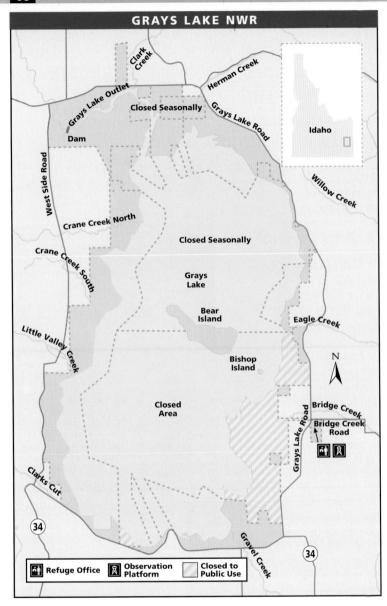

Clark Creek

Herman Creek

Grays Lake Outlet

Closed Seasonally

Grays Lake Road

Idaho

Dam

Willow Creek

West Side Road

Crane Creek North

Closed Seasonally

Crane Creek South

Grays Lake

Bear Island

Eagle Creek

Little Valley Creek

Bishop Island

N

Closed Area

Bridge Creek

Grays Lake Road

Bridge Creek Road

Clarks Cut

34

Gravel Creek

34

| | Refuge Office | | Observation Platform | | Closed to Public Use |

Elevations here range from 6,385 feet on Grays Lake to 9,803 feet atop Caribou Mountain, tallest of the peaks and ridges surrounding the basin. Winters are prolonged and inhumane. In addition to an average yearly snowfall of 115 inches, temperature extremes can reach minus 50 degrees. The last killing frost of the spring generally occurs between May 25 and June 5, though frost is possible any month of the year. Summers are mild, with daytime temperatures rarely exceeding 90 degrees Fahrenheit and cool nights.

■ PLANT LIFE AND HABITATS

Wetlands Grays Lake is very nearly the perfect wetland. About 22,000 acres encompass mosaics of marsh, wet meadow, mudflats, shallow open water, and semiwet meadow. Marsh is the dominant type; inundated flats of broad-leaved cattail, hardstem bulrush, and burr reed form dense, impenetrable thickets. In open water, submergent plants such as pondweed and bladderwort thrive. Wet meadows are lush, spongy reaches of sedges, clovers, and grasses, where water lies at or near ground level most of the year. A bit drier are the semiwet meadows, where the vegetation varies greatly with soil and moisture levels but usually includes sedges and grasses, with sagebrush and rabbit brush occupying the edges and terraces. Also dispersed among these areas are some 225 acres of willow thickets. Refuge managers are working to thin bulrush and cattail stands, which they consider to be too thick and expansive. Ways to increase small openwater areas within the heavy marsh vegetation are being explored.

Arid lands Some 4,000 acres of drier uplands and mountain slopes feature a combination of grasslands, montane shrub, and sagebrush-grasslandcommunities. Grasslands here are used as pasture for livestock or hay production, with tufted hairgrass and Kentucky bluegrass (which actually may be a native species here). Sagebrush-grassland areas include silver and big sage; yarrow and lupine are among the wildflowers. On south- and west-facing slopes at higher elevations are dense tangles of montane shrub, with many species—mountain mahogany, juniper, serviceberry, and chokecherry.

Forests A small portion of the refuge reaches up into aspen-conifer forest, seen most frequently on north- and east-facing slopes, and on Bear Island, in the marsh center. Douglas-fir and, outside the refuge boundary, lodgepole and subalpine fir are interspersed with stands of aspen—some of the state's most expansive aspen parklands occur in this region.

Common yarrow and blossoms

■ **ANIMAL LIFE**

Birds The refuge is famous for sandhill cranes. Beginning in early April, these stately birds arrive in great numbers; as many as 200 pairs will nest on-site, the highest concentration of cranes on the planet. One or two whooping cranes may be present in summer.

The array of marsh-associated species at Grays Lake is rich indeed. Present in summer are the white-faced ibis, American bittern, black tern, Franklin's gull, 16 species of nesting waterfowl—including a few trumpeter swans—as well as the Virginia rail, marsh wren, long-billed curlew, black-necked stilt, and Wilson's phalarope. Six species of swallow nest in the valley and most are easily seen feeding over the marsh.

Raptors love this mixture of forest, mountain, and valley. The golden eagle, prairie falcon, and occasional peregrine falcon are joined by a wealth of hawks—northern goshawk, ferruginous, Swainson's, and northern harrier;

seen occasionally are Cooper's and sharp-shinned hawk, along with osprey and bald eagle.

Shrublands and forests host species large and small: Ruffed grouse and blue grouse nest in the area, as do four species of hummingbird, including the calliope and black-chinned. The diversity of nesting species goes on—mountain chick-adee, black-headed grosbeak, lazuli bunting, green-tailed towhee, mountain blue-bird, Steller's jay, dark-eyed junco, yellow-rumped and orange-crowned warblers are all here.

Mammals With its habitat diversity, Grays Lake's mammal list is commensu-rately rich; opportunities are here for memorable encounters. Moose, muskrat, mink, and beaver ply the marshes and willow thickets. Grasslands and sagebrush are the haunts of many ground squirrels, including the Uinta and Richardson's; long-tailed and short-tailed weasels are present, as are badger, white-tailed jackrab-bit, red fox, and coyote. More elusive species—mountain lion, black bear, elk, and bobcat—prowl in the mountains and forests and are seldom seen. Your chances of spotting porcupine, yellow pine chipmunk, yellow-bellied marmot, least chip-munk, and mountain cottontail rabbit are far better. Elk are more likely to be seen on lands adjoining the refuge. Uncomfirmed sightings of wolves ranging south from Yellowstone continue; it's only a matter of time before they're residents in this remote area.

ACTIVITIES

■ **CAMPING:** Camping is not permitted on the refuge, but the Gravel Creek Campground lies just 9 miles south of refuge headquarters in Caribou National Forest.

■ **SWIMMING:** No swimming is allowed on the refuge.

■ **WILDLIFE OBSERVATION:** Grays Lake is considered a difficult place to view wildlife, but a few tips will help. By July 1, marsh vegetation is fully devel-oped, and many of the birds disappear; visiting between late April and mid-June will greatly improve sightings. After this period, stake out one of two open-water areas: the outlet canal on the north end or Beavertail Point on the south. More-elusive marsh birds are easier to encounter here.

Coyote in grasses

Mountain cottontail

■ **PHOTOGRAPHY:** The overlook at refuge headquarters is ideal for panoramic views of the valley.

■ **HIKES AND WALKS:** Visitors will enjoy the observation platform at refuge headquarters, with interpretive displays, a spotting scope for viewing wildlife, and tremendous panoramic views of the valley. Gravel roads encircling the refuge offer decent vantage points for wildlife observation during the prime months of summer. Refuge roads are the sole option during prime summer months; traffic is scant. A series of unimproved roads on the northeast side of the refuge take visitors through grasslands and wet meadows and approach the marsh.

HUNTING AND FISHING
Hunting is permitted for **geese** and **ducks** Oct. to Jan. **Snipe** hunting is not permitted. There is no fishing on the refuge.

In fall, a walk out to Bear Island on the 2-mile-long causeway is a wonderful experience.

■ **SEASONAL EVENTS:** None.

■ **PUBLICATIONS:** Refuge brochure; bird checklist; special brochure on whooping cranes.

Kootenai NWR
Bonner's Ferry, Idaho

White-tailed deer

Many shades of green adorn 2,774-acre Kootenai NWR, which preserves a meeting place of densely forested mountain foothills with open bottomlands. The result—a blending of marshes and meadows, frothy mountain streams, cool spruce-fir forests, and belts of willow and stately cottonwoods—is as ecologically rich as it is pleasing to the eye.

HISTORY

Conversion of the Kootenai River floodplain to agriculture began in the 1920s; the resulting loss of wetlands and bottomland forests spurred the creation of Kootenai NWR in 1965. Today a system of pumps diverts water from refuge creeks and the Kootenai River into refuge ponds and irrigates food plots for wildlife. In Idaho terms, Kootenai is a popular refuge, with around 20,000 annual visitors.

GETTING THERE

From Sandpoint, Idaho, travel north on US Hwy. 95 30 mi. to the town of Bonner's Ferry; turn left (west) onto Riverside Rd., and travel 5 mi. to refuge entrance.
- **SEASON:** Open year-round.
- **HOURS:** Daylight hours; refuge headquarters: weekdays, 8 a.m.–4:30 p.m.
- **FEES:** None.
- **ADDRESS:** HCR 60, Box 283, Bonner's Ferry, ID 83805
- **TELEPHONE:** 208/267-3888

TOURING KOOTENAI

- **BY AUTOMOBILE:** A 4.5-mile loop-tour route begins at refuge headquarters and circles the major ponds and wetland areas. The tour is open year-round, road conditions permitting.

■ **BY FOOT:** There are tremendous opportunities here for good walking, on more than 5.5 miles of trails, including 2.1-mile Deep Creek Trail, 0.25-mile Myrtle Falls Trail, Cottonwood Trail, the handicapped-accessible Chickadee Trail, along with the Myrtle Pond and Forest trails. Most are open year-round; a few close intermittently during fall hunting season.

■ **BY BICYCLE:** Permitted on refuge auto tour and adjacent county roads; more bike trails are on Idaho Panhandle National Forest lands abutting the refuge to the west.

■ **BY CANOE, KAYAK, OR BOAT:** The Kootenai River forms the eastern boundary of the refuge. There is no boat access on refuge grounds, but opportunities for paddlers exist upstream and downstream. Contact the refuge or the Idaho Panhandle National Forest for more information.

WHAT TO SEE

■ **LANDSCAPE AND CLIMATE** Moist Pacific air, delivering 25 inches of precipitation annually, is an important element of Kootenai's biologically unique region. Tree, shrub, and flower species from the temperate rain forest, northern boreal forest, northern plains, and continental forests of the Rocky Mountains intermingle here in a splendid community known as an inland maritime forest.

The refuge occupies the narrow Kootenai River Valley, bounded by the Selkirk Mountains to the west and the Purcell Range to the east. A raging fury in its natural state, Kootenai River was shackled by Montana's Libby Dam in 1975, to the detriment of at least two native fish species: the white sturgeon and bull trout, listed respectively as endangered and threatened today.

■ **PLANT LIFE AND HABITATS** Of the many ponds here, a majority are classic marsh, with open water and graceful stands of hardstem bulrush. Others, such as Cascade Pond, occupy mountain foothills and are lavishly diverse—sedges, willows, snag trees, and forests of Englemann spruce and Douglas fir hug the edges. Deep and Myrtle creeks tumble through forest to the valley, where they traverse woodlands of cottonwood and alder, forming sloughs and some wet meadows.

Rufous hummingbird

About 200 acres of food plots, primarily grains, are planted and left standing for wildlife.

■ **ANIMAL LIFE**
Birds Forest birds include three grouse species, Cooper's hawk, pileated and black-backed woodpeckers, northern pygmy owl, and many songbirds: chestnut-backed chickadee, veery, Steller's jay, black-headed grosbeak, MacGillivray's and Townsend's warblers, rufous hummingbird, cedar waxwing, red-eyed vireo, and brown creeper.

Mammals Forest wildlife, both winged and furred, is a special attraction at Kootenai. Black bear, moose, elk, mule deer, and white-tailed deer all visit this refuge, especially in spring and fall. Many smaller mammals—pine marten, yellow pine and red-tailed chipmunks, Columbian ground squirrel, and northern flying squirrel—are also present.

Reptiles and amphibians The species here are numerous: Pacific tree frog and wood frog, western toad, and long-toed salamander have been documented, along with the northern alligator lizard, rubber boa, and northern painted turtle.

Fish A total of 22 fish species inhabit refuge streams, ponds, and the Kootenai River.

ACTIVITIES

■ **CAMPING:** Camping is not permitted on the refuge, but there are good options in adjacent Idaho Panhandle National Forest (208/267-5561).

■ **WILDLIFE OBSERVATION AND PHOTOGRAPHY:** There is much to see here, but the opportunity to see birds is especially rewarding. Bald eagles maintain an active nest at Kootenai; wood ducks and owls utilize the numerous nest boxes. The Myrtle Pond observation blind provides superb opportunities to photograph wetland birds and mammals.

■ **HIKES AND WALKS:** No visit to Kootenai is complete without taking the 0.25-mile walk up to beautiful Myrtle Falls, a tumbling 80- to 100-foot cascade in a small, spectacular gorge.

■ **SEASONAL EVENTS:** An International Migratory Bird Day celebration is held in mid-May, with demonstrations, guided birdwatching tours, and children's events.

■ **PUBLICATIONS:** Refuge brochure with map; checklist of all vertebrate species; pictorial guide to common wildlife; Forest Service publications on trees and wildflowers of the region.

Minidoka NWR
Rupert, Idaho

Snake River Plain, Minidoka NWR

The Snake River Plain is a world of near limitless sunshine and vast open spaces, with the beautiful Snake River ever present in the undulating landscape. To know the Snake is to know both the human and natural history of this region, and 20,669-acre Minidoka NWR is an excellent place to get started.

HISTORY

Credit for the word *minidoka* belongs either to the Shoshoni Indians, for whom it meant "wide expanse," a reference to this sweeping Snake River plain, or the Teton Sioux, in which case it translates as "not much water." One of the nation's oldest refuges, Minidoka was established in 1909, three years after completion of the Minidoka Dam, under the direction of President Theodore Roosevelt. Today, about 9,000 people visit Minidoka each year.

GETTING THERE

From the town of American Falls, take I-86 northeast and then take Exit 211 and travel north on ID Hwy. 24, following signs to Lake Walcott State Park through the town of Rupert. Continue north 6 mi. through the town of Acequia, turning right (east) onto County Rd. 400; drive another 6 mi. to parking entrance and refuge headquarters.

■ **SEASON:** Open year-round.

■ **HOURS:** Refuge open during daylight hours; refuge headquarters open weekdays, 8 a.m.–4:30 p.m.

■ **FEES:** User fees at Lake Walcott State Park, within the bounds of the refuge; no fees at refuge.

■ **ADDRESS:** 961 East Minidoka Dam, Rupert, ID 83350-9414

■ **TELEPHONE:** 208/436-3589

TOURING MINIDOKA

■ **BY AUTOMOBILE:** The refuge has no formal auto-tour route. The road that runs along the refuge's north side is driveable, but some roads are open only seasonally and many are better suited for 4-wheel-drive vehicles.

■ **BY FOOT:** There are very good opportunities for walking here, but no designated trails. Cross-country travel is permitted, and unimproved roads—many of which require a 4-wheel-drive vehicle—traverse the length of the refuge along its northern boundary. A short paved trail accessible to wheelchairs is available at Lake Walcott State Park.

■ **BY BICYCLE:** There are relatively few refuge roads open to the public, and trails are rough and better suited for mountain biking. The terrain is rolling, and some unimproved routes require skill to negotiate.

■ **BY CANOE, KAYAK, OR BOAT:** Boating is permitted within designated areas on Lake Walcott and in several "boat lanes" upriver from April 1–September 30; powerboats are best suited for this very large impoundment, though Walcott's irregular north shore, with many bays and inlets, offers paddlers some options.

WHAT TO SEE

■ **LANDSCAPE AND CLIMATE** This is the heart of Idaho's Snake River Plain, long a region of intense volcanic activity. The low, undulating terrain is punctuated with outcrops of lava rock. In this semiarid climate, winter temperatures are mild, with brief periods of subzero readings; summers can be hot, with highs into the 90s followed by cool evenings. Annual precipitation averages about 9 inches. Wildfire occurs annually in this region between late summer and early fall.

The Snake River flows 25 miles through Minidoka refuge, collecting behind a dam to form Lake Walcott, which at 12,000 acres comprises more than half of the refuge. Numerous islands, including two very large ones, Tule and Bird, offer exceptional nesting sites for an impressive array of water-dependent bird species.

■ PLANT LIFE AND HABITATS

Wetlands and woodlands About 2 percent of refuge lands—primarily the shallower inlets of Lake Walcott—feature dense marshes of hardstem bulrush and cattail, with tall stands of crested wheatgrass on the outer margins. Dense thickets of riparian woodlands—willows, Russian olive, and cottonwood—occur in these areas as well. A similar mix of plants graces the islands. Submergent plants such as sago pondweed form expansive beds in shallows on the lake.

Arid lands and grasslands Native shrub-steppe dominates Minidoka's uplands. This unique community of big sagebrush, rubber and green rabbit brush, and wildflowers such as phlox and death camas has been greatly diminished—first through conversion to agriculture and more recently by exotic plants. A nonnative grass, cheatgrass, or downy brome, has badly degraded Minidoka's steppe, outcompeting native Sandberg's bluegrass and needle-and-thread. The refuge continues to burn and reseed some grassland sites in an effort to mitigate the invaders.

■ ANIMAL LIFE

Birds Lake Walcott's abundance of white sucker and carp draws many species of gulls, terns, grebes, herons, and egrets, many of which nest in colonies on refuge islands. Idaho's only nesting population of American white pelicans is here; 40 or more pairs may be readily observed. During migration, rare or accidental species traveling the Pacific Flyway may stop at Minidoka. Eagles are common year-round, balds in winter, goldens spring through fall.

Mammals Notable mammals on this refuge include the river otter, mule deer, yellow-bellied marmot, coyote, and pronghorn.

Reptiles The Great Basin gopher snake, rubber boa, and western yellow-bellied racer are joined by as many as five other species at Minidoka. The pygmy horned lizard, western skink, long-nosed leopard lizard, and western fence lizard are present as well.

Bald eagle

ACTIVITIES

■ **CAMPING:** Lake Walcott State Park, within refuge boundaries, provides camping, but there is no camping on the refuge itself.

■ **SWIMMING:** Swimming is not allowed on the refuge.

■ **WILDLIFE OBSERVATION:** There is good songbird diversity here during spring and fall migrations—wooded areas close to headquarters are productive. Watch for otters near Tule Island. Peregrine falcons have nested on-site, along with lark bunting, grasshopper sparrow, sandhill crane, and short-eared owl.

■ **PHOTOGRAPHY:** There are opportunities for shots of colonial nesting birds and scenic images of the Snake River along the refuge's eastern half.

■ **HIKES AND WALKS:** For solitude and chance encounters with deer, pronghorn, and shrubland songbirds, walk the rugged unimproved road paralleling the Snake River on Minidoka's northern boundary. For a more accessible walk to explore the lakeshore, drive out on Bird Island Road to parking area A; from here, it's a short walk to water's edge, with good viewing of Bird Island and its many feathered inhabitants. Keep in mind that the road is open only seasonally, from September 21 through January 14.

■ **SEASONAL EVENTS:** May: International Migratory Bird Day, guided refuge tours and bird walks.

For information on seasonal tours of Minidoka Dam powerhouse for school groups call the Mindoka Dam (208/436-4187); tours are subject to staff availability.

■ **PUBLICATIONS:** Refuge brochure with map; bird checklist.

Benton Lake NWR
Great Falls, Montana

Camouflaged savannah sparrow

The vista of unbounded prairie was said to have profoundly moved those settlers who first laid eyes upon it. Today, most of the prairielands have been altered, but certain pieces of this remarkable landscape remain. At Benton Lake NWR, towering clouds sail along from west to east, casting a shifting mosaic of shadow and sunlight over the great expanse. A flock of American white pelicans soars high overhead on outstretched wings spanning 9 feet. They pass through a shaft of sunlight, and become spectres, floating pieces of light. It is a moment out of time, a voyage to another era, when the great prairie rolled on into the horizon.

HISTORY

Settlers, like wildlife, were drawn to Benton Lake's water, a rare commodity in the semiarid prairie. In 1885, entrepreneurs attempting to irrigate croplands to the east began work on a massive canal; originating at the lake, a ditch 26 feet deep and 1.5 miles long was excavated before the project went bust. As settlement continued, hunters using the area urged the protection of Benton Lake. The refuge was established in 1929; in 1960, water management took a quantum leap forward with a pump station on Muddy Creek. Dikes were constructed to mediate water levels through dry periods. Refuge roads and facilities appeared at the same time.

GETTING THERE

From Great Falls, drive north on US 87 for 1.0 mi., turn left onto Bootlegger Trail, and continue for 9 mi. Look for sign to refuge headquarters.

- ■ **SEASON:** Open year-round.
- ■ **HOURS:** Open daylight hours; refuge office: Mon.–Fri., 8 a.m.–4:30 p.m.
- ■ **FEES:** None.
- ■ **ADDRESS:** Refuge office: 922 Bootlegger Trail, Great Falls, MT 59404-6133
- ■ **TELEPHONE:** 406/727-7400

TOURING BENTON LAKE

■ **BY AUTOMOBILE:** Prairie Marsh Wildlife Drive, a 9-mile self-guided interpreted tour, is open year-round during daylight hours and traverses refuge grasslands, marshes and open water; the Lower Marsh Road is open July 15 to September 30; all gravel, this road is not recommended for RVs or vehicles pulling trailers.

■ **BY FOOT:** Visitors may hike year-round in all upland areas and on the IV-B Dike from July 15 to September 30. Caution: Rattlesnakes inhabit some areas along and east of Bootlegger Trail. Cross-country skiing is possible throughout the refuge, though access can be limited in winter because of minimal snow conditions.

■ **BY BICYCLE:** Biking is permitted along Prairie Marsh Wildlife Drive.

■ **BY CANOE, KAYAK, OR BOAT:** Canoeing is allowed in the far northwest corner of Benton Lake by special-use permit only. Contact refuge staff for details.

WHAT TO SEE

■ **LANDSCAPE AND CLIMATE** This is a formidable landscape. The northern plains dip and roll into forever. In the distance, in three directions, are mountain ranges: the Highwoods to the east, the Big Belts to the south, and the majestic palisades of the Rocky Mountain Front to the west, where the Great Plains end abruptly against an upthrust wall of stone 10,000 feet high. Glaciers scoured the region east of the Rockies, including the shallow basin that today is Benton Lake.

■ **PLANT LIFE AND HABITATS**

Wetlands Benton Lake is actually a sprawling, shallow marsh; it covers 5,000 acres today. Its water levels vary from a few inches to 6 feet deep. Cattails and bulrushes form thickets and corridors in the open water. Freshwater shrimp and aquatic insect life are prolific. Prior to 1960, the lake depended solely on runoff from the Lake Creek drainage; today Muddy Creek pump station delivers additional water in the form of irrigation returns. The increased water makes it possible to keep marshlands thriving in dry years. The system has a downside, however. Although the "irrigation returns" are of generally good quality, as the water flows through ditches and stream channels to the refuge, it picks up runoff from surrounding farmland—silt, salts, and even more serious contaminants such as selenium. The refuge conducts regular water tests to keep track of selenium levels. After years of study, several management actions are under way to deal with these problems, but progress is slow.

Grasslands About 6,000 acres of Benton Lake's uplands include native shortgrass prairie. Adapted to searing heat, arctic winters, drought, and limitless wind, these ground-hugging grasses and wildflowers may lack the postcard drama of their eastern relative, the tallgrass prairie, but survive they do. When spring rains come in May and June, green needlegrass and wheatgrasses quickly green, milk vetch and scarlet mallow bloom, and the beauty is as intense as it is brief.

Mallard duckling

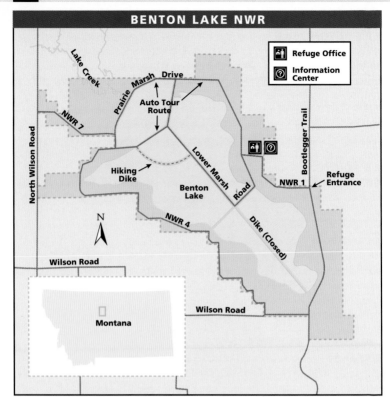

Man-made habitats Dense nesting cover is planted for the benefit of the 12 duck species nesting on-site; other man-made habitats include nesting structures—islands and moats—for Canada geese and ducks. Dike walls, built of broken rock, are inhabited by rodents and other small mammals.

■ **ANIMAL LIFE** Benton Lake is one of the country's most prolific waterfowl breeding sites. In a good year, some 40,000 ducks—the progeny of mallards, gadwall, northern pintail, lesser scaup, northern shoveler, redhead, ruddy duck, canvasback, and three teal species—are born and raised here. Suffice it to say that a visit in June will yield sightings of more than a few downy ducklings.

The mudflats, wet meadows, and grassland fringes also support a diversity of shorebirds. The refuge has been recognized by the Western Hemisphere Shorebird Reserve Network as an important site for nesting and migratory shorebirds. Black-necked stilt, American avocet, long-billed curlew and marbled godwit nest at Benton Lake. During migration, many species appear in varying numbers—greater and lesser yellowlegs, Baird's sandpiper, short-billed dowitcher, semipalmated plover, pectoral sandpiper, and, on rare occasions, whimbrel, stilt sandpiper, and ruddy turnstone.

Joining the waterfowl and shorebirds are a variety of other prairie marsh regulars—the black tern, sora rail, eared and pied-billed grebe, black-crowned night-heron, marsh wren, yellow-headed blackbird, and white-faced ibis. All nest on the refuge.

Migration at Benton Lake is a spectacle. It starts in mid-March, when ducks and several thousand tundra swans arrive; next are the snow geese, also numbering in the hundreds or thousands. The arrival of shorebirds marks the end of the show. In fall the progression is more or less reversed, beginning in late August with shorebirds and culminating in late October with ducks and swans. Shadowing the flocks are the raptors—the bald eagle, Swainson's hawk, peregrine falcon, golden eagle, gyrfalcon, and prairie falcon. Visitors who are patient and spend a day or two in the field may witness one of these winged carnivores taking a meal.

In the grasslands are native songbirds, particularly sparrows. Usually heard more often than seen are the Baird's, lark, grasshopper, and savannah sparrows. The beautiful chestnut-collared longspur is often seen; the McCown's longspur is present but less common. A few burrowing owls nest here in summer.

Small numbers of pronghorn antelope and white-tailed deer move in and out of refuge holdings; the coyote, badger, raccoon, and white-tailed jackrabbit are present but elusive.

ACTIVITIES

■ **CAMPING AND SWIMMING:** No camping or swimming is allowed on Benton refuge. Camping facilities are available in privately owned campgrounds in nearby Great Falls, 15 miles away.

■ **WILDLIFE OBSERVATION:** With so many ducks, grebes, and other water-fowl here, it helps to know a few basics of identification. Ducks fall into two major groups, dabblers and divers. Dabblers, which include most of the nesting species at Benton Lake, can spring from a resting position directly into flight. Diving ducks, along with other waterbirds such as grebes, loons, cormorants, and mergansers (all seen here at different times), need a running start—they patter across the water to build up speed for takeoff. Also note the profile of the bird as it swims; most divers ride appreciably lower in the water than dabblers.

■ **PHOTOGRAPHY:** The refuge encourages photographers to visit, though it also seeks to minimize the stress of human encounters on nesting birds. A special-use permit is required; the process takes just five minutes, and refuge staff are happy to provide tips on where and how to photograph refuge wildlife with the best results.

> **HUNTING AND FISHING**
> Hunting is permitted for **waterfowl** and upland birds, including **ring-necked pheasant**, **gray partridge**, and **sharp-tailed grouse**. There is no big game hunting allowed. There is no fishing on the refuge; waters are too shallow for fish to survive the winter freeze-up.

■ **HIKES AND WALKS:** Refuge roads provide the best access for seeing wildlife; hiking options are limited to these routes and to the mile-long trail off Lower Marsh Road. Views of wildlife along the trail are no better; Stop 8 on the auto-tour route offers the best overview of the lake and surrounding lands.

■ **SEASONAL EVENTS:** None.

■ **PUBLICATIONS:** Refuge guide; tour-route brochure; bird list; public-use activity list.

Bowdoin NWR
Malta, Montana

Lake Bowdoin alkali deposits, Bowdoin NWR

Out here in what is called the "big empty," an 8-inch ground squirrel standing upright can survey a great expanse of terrain and become a distinct element in that terrain—it's not called shortgrass prairie by accident. This is the setting for the 15,550-acre Bowdoin National Wildlife Refuge, a prairie oasis.

HISTORY

The region's prairie rivers and wetlands have long been susceptible to outbreaks of botulism, which develops when receding lakes or wetlands bake under the extreme heat of a northern plains summer. Massive die-offs of waterfowl and shorebirds can result. When Bowdoin was established in 1936, controlling these outbreaks has been a priority since then. A series of dikes built on the Milk River provides Lake Bowdoin and its adjacent wetlands with freshwater throughout the year.

GETTING THERE

From Malta, drive 1 mi. northeast on US 2 and turn right onto County Rd. 2 (also known as Old Hwy. 2). Proceed 6 mi. to refuge headquarters, located on the right, at Lake Bowdoin.
- **SEASON:** Open year-round.
- **HOURS:** Daylight hours.
- **FEES:** None.
- **ADDRESS:** HC 65, P.O. Box 5700, Malta, MT 59538
- **TELEPHONE:** 406/654-2863

TOURING BOWDOIN

- **BY AUTOMOBILE:** A 15-mile self-guided auto tour encircles Lake Bowdoin; the route is open year-round unless roads become impassable due to wet weather or snow.

■ **BY FOOT:** Hiking is possible near the auto-tour route, though no designated trails have been constructed. Hiking in closed areas requires a special-use permit.

■ **BY BICYCLE:** Biking is allowed on the auto-tour route only.

■ **BY CANOE, KAYAK, OR BOAT:** Canoes and boats with a maximum engine of 10 hp may use parts of Lake Bowdoin and the Drumbo Unit during the fall waterfowl hunt.

WHAT TO SEE

■ **LANDSCAPE AND CLIMATE** This reach of the northern plains lies at 2,209 feet—and that's about it. Elevations change just 80 feet across the entire refuge. Winds sweep the prairie year-round, delivering occasional blasts of extreme cold during winter and sweltering heat in late summer. Precipitation totals 12 inches annually. Lake Bowdoin originated as a massive horseshoe bend in the preglacial Missouri River, which shifted its course about 50 miles south of Bowdoin during the Ice Age.

■ **PLANT LIFE AND HABITATS**

Wetlands Lake Bowdoin, at 4,000 acres, is a vast prairie marsh; depths range from just 3 to 4 feet and vary by season. The lake's alkaline waters support abundant freshwater shrimp, aquatic insect life, and large beds of sago pondweed, with emergent plants such as alkali and hardstem bulrushes along the margins. Several islands provide ideal nesting sites for great numbers of colonial, or nesting, birds—in an average year, 2,000 American white pelican nests are established on the refuge. At the center of Lake Bowdoin's horseshoe shape is Big Island, which is actually a large peninsula of prairie and invading Russian olive trees. On Woody Island, great blue herons nest on the ground, a very unusual thing to see. Surrounding Lake Bowdoin are two more large, shallow marshes of similar composition. Dry Lake Unit is a large salty wetland. Lakeside Unit and a series of much smaller constructed ponds feature less alkaline waters; they can be controlled and flushed each year to eliminate salt/calcium buildup.

Mink

Grasslands Western wheatgrass, June grasses, and blue grama are dominant in the roughly 6,700 acres of native shortgrass prairie at Bowdoin. Club moss grows here in large, ground-hugging mats and "knobs." Cacti include the prickly pear and tiny pincushion cactus, which produces beautiful magenta flowers in summer. Other wildflowers gracing the prairie—a delight to visitors' eyes—include fringed sagewort, sweet clover, prairie phlox, and scarlet globe mallow. Sagebrush is less abundant at Bowdoin, and most wildlife species associated with it, such as sage grouse, are here in equally limited numbers.

Arid lands Depressions and other low-lying areas at Bowdoin collect heavy concentrations of salts and calcium from the soil. These "saline flats" feature a mix of salt grass and greasewood; the latter is a dense, 3- to 4-foot-high shrub with fleshy leaves and smooth, gray bark. Though they appear raw and desiccated, saline flats attract ground-nesting waterfowl, and songbirds find shelter and food in the greasewood thickets.

Man-made habitats Shelterbelts and planted nesting cover make up 2,000 acres; Russian olive and cottonwood trees, along with shrubs such as chokecherry and buffalo berry, are typical nesting cover species, primarily benefitting neotropical songbirds and raptors.

■ **ANIMAL LIFE** Bowdoin hosts as rich a diversity of wild species as can be found across the northern plains. Its colonial nesting birds—pelicans, California, ring-billed and Franklin's gulls, white-faced ibis, Caspian terns, double-crested cormorants, among others—are common here in dense concentrations from spring through late summer. Some 15 duck species nest on-site, including the canvasback, American wigeon, and common goldeneye. Along marsh edges and into grasslands are many elegant shorebirds—the black-necked stilt, American avocet, marbled godwit, piping plover, willet, and long-billed curlew all nest here. The piping plover, however, is barely hanging in there: About 1 to 2 pairs of these threatened birds nest at Bowdoin, and refuge biologists frequently monitor brood success and coordinate with local irrigation and grazing districts if a nest warranting protection turns up outside refuge boundaries.

Many visitors come in search of grassland songbirds—the Baird's sparrows, chestnut-collared and McCown's longspurs, and Sprague's pipit. The loggerhead shrike is common in summer. In March and April bald eagles make their appearance, with as many as 70 to 150 birds passing through. Golden eagles and prairie falcons are commonly seen; in winter, reliable numbers of rough-legged hawks and northern goshawks appear to hunt the refuge. The Swainson's and ferruginous hawks nest on-site.

Mink and muskrat inhabit the bulrush thickets and quieter inlets of the marsh and are seen occasionally in morning and evening. Bowdoin supports one of the area's largest herds of white-tailed deer (about 250); they graze refuge lands and surrounding agricultural fields.

American avocet, Bowdoin NWR

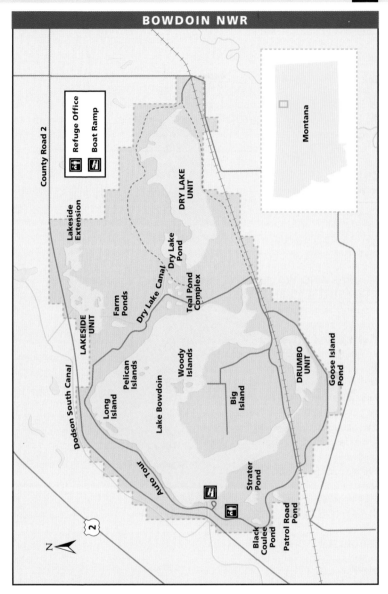

A few reptiles and amphibians eke out a living here. Snakes, such as the prairie rattlesnake, bull snake, and eastern yellow-bellied racer, are present. The eastern short-horned lizard is probably here, though its status is not well known. Boreal chorus frogs and northern leopard frogs inhabit the marshes and sing to prospective mates in April and May.

The prairie community features a herd of nearly 200 pronghorn antelope, plus such burrowers as the Richardson's ground squirrel and badger. Coveys of sharp-tailed grouse and pheasant skitter through the grasses and along road edges.

Bowdoin is to serve as a breeding and preconditioning facility for black-footed ferrets prior to their reintroduction at other sites in the state. The first batch of kits was due to arrive in mid-1999. Living in a large enclosure, the kits will be "preconditioned" for release into the wild—meaning they will learn to catch and eat black-tailed prairie dogs, their primary prey.

ACTIVITIES

■ **CAMPING:** No camping is allowed on the refuge, but Malta and Nelson Reservoir, about 12 miles northeast, have commercial camping facilities.

■ **SWIMMING:** No swimming is allowed at Bowdoin refuge.

■ **WILDLIFE OBSERVATION:** Each season offers opportunities to see wildlife—most notably birds—and some are birds not easily encountered elsewhere in the region. Serious birders pay attention to Bowdoin's shorebird migrations in spring and fall and visit from all over the country to see its grassland songbirds.

■ **PHOTOGRAPHY:** Sunrise over Lake Bowdoin is a splendid sight, especially in spring and summer, when all manner of birds are on the move over its misty waters—the refuge road north of headquarters offers good vantage points. Big Island is a good site for images of pronghorn, prairie flowers, and, closer to the edge of the lake, nesting birds traveling to and from Woody and South Woody islands.

■ **HIKES AND WALKS:** Visitor use at Bowdoin has increased in recent years (now exceeding 5,000), and the days when a visitor could walk anywhere without inquiring at headquarters are over. The refuge management is currently reassessing guidelines for hiking and walking in the area; visitors interested in walking cross-country should talk with staff before setting out. One very satisfying hike would be a trek across Big Island, the grassland peninsula jutting out into Lake Bowdoin. Pronghorn favor this area, as do many other grassland species. From the refuge road to the far shore of the peninsula, it's roughly a 3-mile walk. There are no walking trails, though a two-track refuge road accesses the east side of the peninsula.

> **HUNTING AND FISHING** Hunting is permitted for **waterfowl** and upland birds, including **ring-necked pheasant, sharp-tailed grouse**, and **gray partridge**. No big-game hunting is allowed. There is no fishing on the refuge.

■ **SEASONAL EVENTS:** The refuge celebrates International Migratory Bird Day on May 8 and a Bowdoin National Wildlife Refuge Christmas Bird Count.

■ **PUBLICATIONS:** Refuge brochures; bird list; mammal list; public-use regulations; auto-tour route leaflet.

Charles M. Russell NWR
Lewistown, Montana

Missouri Breaks, Charles M. Russell NWR

From Lewis and Clark to Charlie Russell, no one has ever passed through this monumental landscape unimpressed. It unrolls over miles and miles, a labyrinth of steep, eroded canyons, mesas and arroyos, sweeping plateaus of prairie grasslands, with ridges, coulees, and basins cloaked in fir and pine—the Missouri Breaks.

Meandering through a floodplain of cottonwood and willow forests, the Missouri River pushes eastward, its depth and powerful current concealed beneath a glassy surface. Herds of elk, bighorn sheep, and pronghorn graze the grasslands and the high, desiccated ridges. Sage grouse. prairie dogs, and bobcats roam here. Blazing sun bakes the rock spires; sparkling streams hide in steep drainages. Encompassing 1.1 million acres (1,718 square miles, almost the size of Delaware) of some of the wildest, most untouched country in the United States, Charles M. Russell NWR (CMR) could be visited every week for a lifetime, and there would still be more to see.

HISTORY

Refuge history is tame; settlement history is something else. Fur traders and buffalo hunters gave way to steamboat commerce and a very rough frontier community of horse thieves, whiskey traders, gun-toting outlaws like Kid Curry, and vigilante posses like Stuart's Stranglers. Numerous homesteads can be found on refuge lands; three Lewis and Clark campsites have been identified from their original journals.

Renowned naturalist Adolph Murie conducted a biological survey of this region in 1935, and the Fort Peck Game Range was established a year later. In 1963 the "range" was renamed to honor Charles M. Russell, the legendary Montana artist whose paintings recorded the people and landscapes of this rugged place. The U.S. Fish & Wildlife Service assumed sole management of the site in 1976. Today, close to 60,000 people visit this refuge every year.

GETTING THERE

From Lewistown travel north on US 191 for 70 miles to the Fred Robinson Bridge spanning the Missouri River; refuge lands begin on the north side of the river. From Fort Peck, refuge lands to the west are accessed by following the Willow Creek South Rd.; to reach refuge lands to the south, use MT 24.

- **SEASON:** Open year-round.
- **HOURS:** Dawn to dusk.
- **FEES:** None.
- **ADDRESS:** P.O. Box 110, Airport Rd., Lewistown, MT 59457-0110
- **TELEPHONE:** 406/538-8707

TOURING CHARLES M. RUSSELL

■ **BY AUTOMOBILE:** Refuge roads include well maintained routes and back-country two-tracks; some roads are closed seasonally; check with refuge head-quarters. A high-clearance or 4WD vehicle is an asset. CMR's 20-mile self-guided auto tour is accessible to most any vehi-cle; the route is well-maintained and provides an excellent overview of the refuge and its wildlife. All roads deteri-orate rapidly in rain or snow and become impassable until they dry out.

■ **BY FOOT:** Hiking is allowed throughout the refuge year-round, including the 20,000-acre UL Bend Wilderness area, a separate refuge. There are no designated trails on the refuge itself, though visitors will dis-cover jeep roads and game trails criss-crossing many lands. Several footpaths begin along the auto-tour route and offer leisurely exploration. Experience with map and compass is recom-mended for exploring the more remote areas. Carry in your own water.

■ **BY BICYCLE:** All numbered routes on the refuge are open to bicycles, but check with refuge headquarters for advice about roads passable to bikes.

Lupine

The landscape is extremely rugged and varied, with open flats cut by steep ravines and drainages; for visitors in decent shape and possessed of good backcountry skills, cycling here can be an unforget-table experience.

■ **BY CANOE, KAYAK, OR BOAT:** Bisecting the heart of CMR, the Mis-souri River is a boater's paradise in summer and early fall. Some 135 miles of the "Mo" are designated "Wild and Scenic," giving this section special protec-tion, including a sizable portion of CMR's western half. Many floaters put in well upriver of the refuge and use the Fred Robinson Bridge on MT 191 as their takeout; it's also possible to put in at Robinson and journey 10 miles downriver to the Rock Creek Boat Access, a concrete ramp located on the north side of the river.

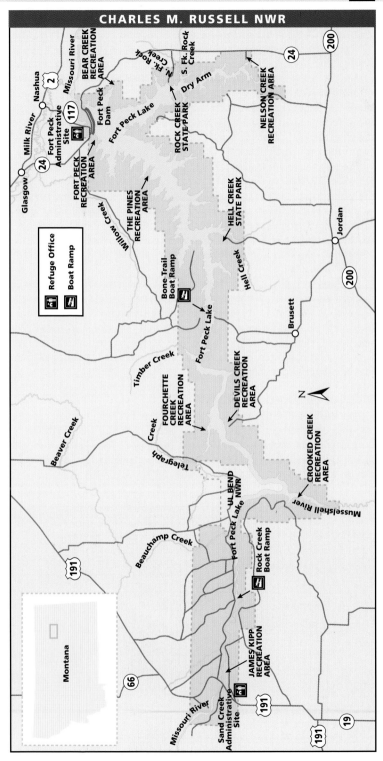

CHARLES M. RUSSELL NWR

WHAT TO SEE

■ LANDSCAPE AND CLIMATE CMR's raw, dramatic landscape emerged 15,000 years ago when advancing glaciers from Canada blocked the Missouri River's ancient route to the Hudson Bay. Inundating much of the northern reaches of the refuge, melting glacial waters carted off layer after layer of earth, carving deep fissures and ravines in the soft sedimentary layers of shale, mudstone, and sandstone. The resulting formations, known as the Missouri Breaks, are an inverted mountain range of sorts: Tabletop lands occupy much of the horizon, with tremendously varied relief hidden below. Wind and extreme temperatures, along with numerous creeks and seasonal floods, are further dissecting the landscape today.

Precipitation in this semiarid climate averages just 13 inches annually, with 70 percent of it arriving between April and September. May and June are typically the wettest months; in July and August, afternoon temperatures reach the 80s, and readings as high as 100 are not uncommon. September and early October bring a mixture of fast-moving rain or snow squalls and stretches of clear blue skies and daytime temperatures in the 70s, with frosty nights. Winter days are typically sunny and cold, with below-zero temperatures possible from early November through March.

The eastern half of CMR is dominated by a human construct of staggering proportions—the Fort Peck Reservoir on the Missouri River. Built between 1933 and 1940 at a cost of $150 million, it is the largest earthen dam in the nation. Stretching four miles across the valley, the 135-mile-long reservoir created 1,500 miles of shoreline, most of which is extremely rugged and remote. The dam collects water from an estimated one-third of the state, generating hydropower and providing irrigation and flood control.

■ PLANT LIFE AND HABITATS

Open waters The Missouri River is the pulse of CMR, muddy and raging in spring, sluggish and warm by late summer. The free-flowing portion of the river is a stronghold for the paddlefish, a bizarre prehistoric species that swims with mouth agape, feeding on plankton. Its body features cartilage and no bones; the fish are giants, ranging from 40 to more than 100 pounds. Another prehistoric marvel, the endangered pallid sturgeon, is dwindling in numbers, a casualty of lost

Paddlefish, Fort Peck Lake, Charles M. Russell NWR

river current when the Missouri was impounded. The Mussellshell River enters the Missouri at UL Bend; it too is swathed in a verdant belt of deciduous forest and shrubs and, depending on water levels, carves a rich, muddy delta attractive to shorebirds and other species.

Numerous creeks drain the uplands both north and south of the Missouri, among them Seven Blackfeet, Devils, Snow, and Hell.

Fort Peck Reservoir is a superb fishery of walleye, smallmouth bass, and northern pike, although contending with weather conditions and the mazelike shoreline demands experience and planning.

Arid lands The uplands of CMR—nearly 60 percent of the refuge—are a mixture of sagebrush grasslands and northern shortgrass prairie, with species such as little bluestem, needle-and-thread, prickly pear cactus, and western wheatgrasses. Needle-and-thread is so-named for is seedhead, which has a long tail that curves, so that the seed looks like a needle, and the tail resembles the thread. A lively mixture of wildflowers paints hillsides and ridges, especially with the first drenching rains of spring and early summer. Phloxes, yarrow, lupine, arrowleaf balsam, and pasqueflowers are typical species. Pasqueflower is a wild crocuslike flower with a yellow center and six pretty white petals.

Forests Nearly one-third of the refuge is cloaked in a coniferous pine-fir forest, with Douglas fir, ponderosa pine, and Rocky Mountain juniper, plus a scattering of limber pine. Occupying hillsides, coulees, and the bottoms of ravines and steep draws, these forests provide shade, nesting sites, and protective cover for a broad range of wildlife, and they hold fragile soils in place.

The broad floodplain and islands of the Missouri River support a bountiful deciduous bottomland forest of black cottonwood, green ash, and willow. Here the forest understory features shrubs such as hawthorn, chokecherry, and wild rose. Snag trees provide important nesting and roosting sites for both great blue herons and bald eagles. The Mussellshell River, too, features a verdant belt of forest; along Rock and Hell creeks are shady riparian corridors of willow, dogwood, and serviceberry.

Clark's nutcracker

■ ANIMAL LIFE

Birds The beautiful western tanager (red face, with a yellow-black body) is among the 240 bird species recorded here, along with lazuli bunting, northern oriole, and mountain bluebird. The raucous Clark's nutcracker is widespread, as are two native gallinacious birds, the sharp-tailed grouse and sage grouse. The males of both grouse species perform outlandish courtship dances in early spring, gathering on leks, or dancing grounds, and spinning, stomping, and popping their colorful air sacs in an effort to attract a mate. Raptors are another treat at CMR: Golden eagles, ferruginous hawks, prairie falcons and merlins all nest on the refuge. Bald eagles and Swainson's hawks are commonly sighted as well.

Mammals Though the region is vast and remote, a number of the area's more significant mammals—bison, plains elk, wolves, grizzly bears, the Audubon bighorn sheep—were extirpated (or, in the case of the latter, eliminated) during settlement. Restoration efforts in the 1950s and '60s brought indigenous Rocky

Black-footed ferret

Mountain elk and bighorn sheep back to CMR. Both herds have done well: The elk herd numbers roughly 5,000 head, the bighorns about 160. Along with two other plains natives, the mule deer and pronghorn, refuge lands are today filled with hoofprints.

A present-day restoration effort involving the rare black-footed ferret is progressing, albeit slowly. Some 127 ferrets have been reintroduced since 1994, primarily in the UL Bend Wilderness area. In December of 1998 the surviving population was estimated at 40, including 13 litters of at least 38 kits born in the wild during 1999. Survival rates are low, just 20 to 30 percent, an indication of the difficulty of reestablishing a self-sustaining population.

CMR was an easy choice for ferret reintroduction given its thriving population of black-tailed prairie dogs, the ferret's meal of choice. These charming and highly social members of the squirrel family have seen their numbers plummet throughout the West, though they once were a keystone of prairie ecology. CMR is home to perhaps 100 prairie dog "towns," occupying 6,000 acres, most of them on the north side of the Missouri River. Dog towns are a wildlife focal point—burrowing owls, coyotes, rattlesnakes, bobcats, and badgers are never far away. The refuge is also home to the poisonous prairie rattlesnake and the nonpoisonous bull snakes, as well as tiger salamanders, horned lizards, and leopard frogs.

ACTIVITIES

■ **CAMPING:** The entire refuge is open to camping except for a small wildlife viewing area near Highway 191; direct access by motor vehicle is allowed to and from temporary campsites within 100 yards of numbered routes. Developed campsites are available at James Kipp Recreation Area, Rock Creek Boat Ramp, as well as at Crooked Creek, Devils Creek, Forchette Bay, Hell Creek, The Pines,

Nelson Creek, McGuire Creek, Bear Creek, and Fort Peck recreation areas. Ground fires are permitted, but caution should be exercised. Drinking water is scarce and should be packed in.

■ **SWIMMING:** Swimming is permitted within refuge boundaries in the Missouri River and Fort Peck Reservoir.

■ **WILDLIFE OBSERVATION:** CMR's auto tour, which takes about two hours to complete, begins in riverbottom forest and ascends into the breaks; along this route it is possible to sample much of the refuge's wildlife. A wide array of songbirds inhabits the forested riverbottom from mid-May through early August; white-tailed deer and beaver may be glimpsed here year-round. Sharp-tailed grouse often scurry along the margins of the road, with mule deer, pronghorn, and the occasional loping coyote visible on adjacent hillsides and the edges of timbered coulees. Raptors may be encountered in flight most anywhere. Elk are present in an adjacent viewing area in September and October.

Despite their size and abundance, elk often require effort to observe; visitors in fall, however, will be assured of hearing the long, plaintive "bugle" of a rutting bull, an otherworldly call audible for miles. Elk in sizable numbers also gather along the riverbottom during winter and are frequently sighted in other areas of CMR, including the Larb Hills and Harper's Ridge.

Bighorn sheep inhabit the eastern portion of the refuge and may be sighted in the Mickey-Brandon Buttes area. Large numbers of sage grouse and pronghorn occupy the UL Bend refuge area in winter.

■ **PHOTOGRAPHY:** From dawn to dusk, CMR is a photographer's paradise. History buffs will find turn-of-the-century bunkhouses and homestead sites; landscape shutterbugs should explore Iron Stake Ridge and, on the eastern end of the refuge, the Sand Arroyo Badlands. Atop any of the high ridges north of the Missouri, vistas stretch for hundreds of miles—there's absolutely nothing

Elk (wapiti)

between the refuge and Canada—with the large, meandering river a ribbon of blue; low-light situations cast the toothy ridges, coulees, and canyons into dramatic relief and are best for capturing the delicate colors and layers of rock formations.

■ **HIKES AND WALKS:** From leisurely day hikes to weeklong backcountry treks, hiking opportunities at CMR seem virtually endless. Refuge roads offer hikers a terrific experience. Another plus: With more than a million acres to hike and largely seasonal visita-

HUNTING AND FISHING The refuge permits big-game hunting including: **pronghorn antelope**, **mule deer**, **white-tailed deer**, and **elk**. The hunting of **bighorn sheep, pronghorn,** and **elk** is by permit only. **Waterfowl**, **upland birds** (primarily sharp-tailed grouse), and **coyote** hunting is also allowed.

Many species are here—**catfish**, **walleye**, **northern pike**, **sauger**, **perch, smallmouth bass, bullhead**, **paddlefish**, and **lake trout**—in the Missouri River and downstream in sprawling Fort Peck Lake.

tion, traffic can be thin. A few possibilities in the UL Bend area are noted here. A walk through the Hawley Flat area, near the junction of Refuge roads 219 and 319, takes visitors past a black-footed ferret reintroduction site and a sprawling prairie dog town, where a host of other species may be seen. Visitors interested in working up a sweat can drive to the end of Refuge Road 418, then hike to the top of either Brandon (2 miles) or Mickey Butte (0.5 mile), each an inspiring place, with panoramic views and opportunities for sighting bighorn sheep.

■ **SEASONAL EVENTS:** None.

■ **PUBLICATIONS:** Checklists of birds (including the history of the trumpeter swan at Red Rock), along with maps, at refuge headquarters.

Lee Metcalf NWR
Stevensville, Montana

Bitterroot Mountains from Lee Metcalf NWR

The Bitterroot Mountains make a formidable backdrop for this tangled landscape of verdant forest, towering nearly 10,000 feet above Metcalf. But if mountains represent all that is distant and often harsh, this small refuge, with its lush woods fringing the glittering Bitterroot River, is an intimate, inviting place. While the mountains appear solemn and silent, the valley and this refuge reverberate with life.

HISTORY

In 1963, residents of the Bitterroot Valley recognized the finite amount of wild lands here and established the 2,800-acre Ravalli National Wildlife Refuge with funds from the sale of Federal Duck Stamps. Montana Senator Lee Metcalf, a life-long conservationist, was instrumental in shepherding the refuge proposal through Congress, and, in 1978, Ravalli was renamed in the late senator's honor. The vision of those original residents was all too accurate, as today the valley is an increasingly hectic place. It's hard to believe, but Metcalf will one day become an *urban* wildlife refuge. Today it attracts close to 60,000 visitors each year.

GETTING THERE

From Missoula, travel south on US 93 for 25 mi.; turn left onto Stevi Cutoff Rd. (Hwy. 264) and continue 1.0 mi. into Stevensville; turn left onto Eastside Hwy. (Hwy. 203) in Stevensville. Continue 0.25 mi. to Wildfowl Lane and the refuge boundary.

■ **SEASON:** Refuge open year-round.

■ **HOURS:** Refuge and Bitterroot Recreation Area open daylight hours.

■ **FEES:** None.

■ **ADDRESS:** Refuge Headquarters, 115 W. Third St., Stevensville, MT 59870; office hours, 8 a.m.–4:30 p.m., Mon.–Fri. Mail: P.O. Box 267, Stevensville, MT 59870

■ **TELEPHONE:** 406/777-5552; fax 406/777-4344

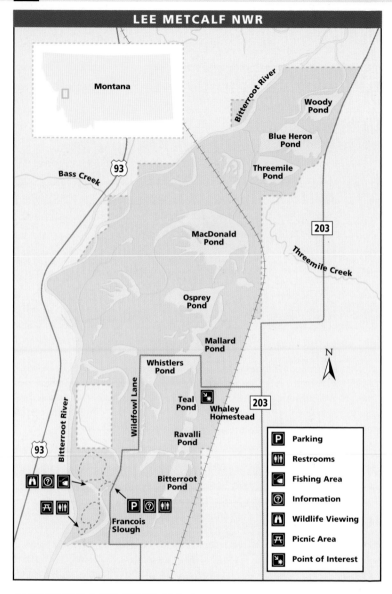

LEE METCALF NWR

Montana

Bitterroot River

Woody
Pond

Blue Heron
Pond

Threemile
Pond

Bass Creek

93

203

Threemile Creek

MacDonald
Pond

Osprey
Pond

Mallard
Pond

Whistlers
Pond

Teal
Pond

Whaley
Homestead

203

Ravalli
Pond

Bitterroot River

93

Bitterroot
Pond

Francois
Slough

N

| P | Parking |
| Restrooms |
| Fishing Area |
| Information |
| Wildlife Viewing |
| Picnic Area |
| Point of Interest |

TOURING LEE METCALF

■ **BY AUTOMOBILE:** Wildfowl Lane, a gravel road bisecting the refuge for about 2.5 miles, offers year-round access.

■ **BY FOOT:** Two miles of trails traverse the 140-acre Bitterroot River Recreation Area, part of the refuge; Wildfowl Lane (2.5 miles) may also be walked.

■ **BY BICYCLE:** Bicycling is permitted along Wildfowl Lane. Eastside Highway is a narrow, winding paved route through the heart of the Bitterroot Valley; it begins in the town of Stevensville and continues north for 11 miles to Florence, Montana.

■ **BY CANOE, KAYAK, OR BOAT:** No boating is allowed on Lee Metcalf refuge. The Bitterroot River, in the recreation area, however, is a popular canoeing, kayaking, and fishing destination; there are numerous public-access points along US 93 between Missoula and Hamilton. Canoe rentals in Missoula.

WHAT TO SEE

■ **LANDSCAPE AND CLIMATE** The Bitterroot Valley is bounded on the west by the Bitterroot Mountains and to the east by the gentler rolling foothills of the Sapphire Range. The influence of warm, moisture-laden Pacific air is felt here; temperatures year-round are considerably milder than just east of the Continental Divide. Annual precipitation averages just 11 inches. The valley lies at an elevation of 3,300 feet, not high for these parts. Just a few miles west, Saint Mary's Peak rises from the valley floor to a height of 9,700 feet.

■ PLANT LIFE AND HABITATS

Open waters The Bitterroot River receives snowmelt from its namesake mountains, looming along the Montana-Idaho border. Glance at this river—its jade-tinted waters and brilliant graveled bottom—and you will know it is a vigorous waterway. Aquatic insect life is varied, and the river supports a thriving trout population, including the native cutthroat. The river's logjams, brushy banks, and secluded side channels provide lush riparian habitat for nesting and migrating songbirds, as well as a variety of aquatic mammals. Its springtime torrents disperse willow, cottonwood, and other seeds over islands and streamside areas, sowing future generations of trees.

Wetlands Permanent wetlands make up about 600 acres and include developed wetlands, the water levels of which can be manipulated, along with a labyrinth of natural sloughs, oxbows, and ponds; these are recharged each spring when the Bitterroot River, swollen with snowmelt, plows through low-lying forested areas. Developed wetlands are bounded by extensive stands of cattails with scattered snag trees, log piles, and other natural detritus utilized by wildlife. Nesting and migratory waterfowl favor these areas, as do a number of nesting marshland songbirds.

Forests Metcalf's centerpiece habitat is 1,800 acres of pristine lowland deciduous forest. Mature black cottonwoods push the canopy high above; these trees are well dispersed, giving the forest an inviting, spacious feel. Soils of the forest floor, covered in leaf litter, are well drained and dry out quickly. Willow, hawthorn, and alder are other important tree species. Thickets of fruit-producing shrubs such as woods rose, red osier dogwood, snowberry and serviceberry provide an important food source for numerous birds, rodents, and white-tailed deer. Also here is one of this refuge's (and the valley's) signature species—scattered stands of majestic ponderosa pines, a somewhat unusual species in this forest type. Look for its rather stiff, curved, darkish green needles, usually in bunches of two or three, each about 6 inches long. The tree has a wide, conical crown and pinkish-brown bark.

Serviceberry

Grasslands No true grasslands are found here, although drier forested sites feature scattered remnants of native palouse-prairie bunchgrasses and wildflowers, including yarrow and blanket flower.

Man-made habitats About 200 acres of the refuge consist of croplands on irrigated and subirrigated uplands. Local farmers leave standing about 70 percent of each year's cereal crop to provide cover and forage for wildlife.

■ **ANIMAL LIFE** The Bitterroot Valley's hourglass shape brings a high diversity of migrating birds to Metcalf; it serves a migration corridor between mountain ranges. Among them are neotropical songbirds. Many warbler species, along with fly-

MIGRATORY BIRD MOTEL Ever seen Canada geese nesting in tall trees? This downright weird occurrence is common at Metcalf and has seldom been documented elsewhere. Up to 20 or so pairs of geese arrive in early spring and commandeer nesting platforms and established natural nests built by unsuspecting ospreys. By the time the downy yellow goslings of these geese hop or flutter to the ground in May or June, the ospreys have arrived and are paired off and ready to raise their own young. The geese move out, the osprey move in.

catchers, vireos, and swifts, descend upon the forests and open fields. Tundra swans, redheads, American wigeon, and ruddy ducks are among the dozens of waterfowl species passing through in early spring. Shorebirds, too, make their appearance: The Wilson's phalarope, long-billed dowitcher, and snipe are common; the black-bellied plover, greater and lesser yellowlegs, and Baird's sandpiper are seen less frequently.

Snag trees are common in Metcalf's lowland forests, as are living trees with sheared-off tops or fractured limbs; the result is a mecca for woodpeckers and owls. Six species of woodpecker (including the pileated and Lewis') have been sighted, along with seven owl species, the long-eared, western screech-owl, and northern saw-whet among them. A pair of great horned owls maintain a nest in the Bitterroot River Recreation Area. Other nesting birds in the forest include the black-headed grosbeak, veery, American redstart, and common yellowthroat.

American wigeons, female and male

In marshes, ponds, and along the Bitterroot River, visitors may encounter beaver, muskrat, mink, or, with a bit of luck, the charismatic river otter. Noisy kingfishers ply the river and ponds for a meal, as do great blue herons. The occasional cow moose, sometimes with calf in tow, appears during summer to browse willows and dogwood along sloughs and oxbows. Listen for Yellow-headed blackbirds commandeer the cattails for their breeding territories, the colorful males issuing their cheery, toy-horn call. Osprey utilize snag trees

Osprey with fish, Lee Metcalf NWR

and man-made platforms for their nests; it is not possible to visit without seeing a pair or two tending their nests along Wildfowl Lane in summer. A pair of bald eagles have nested here for seven years; their haunts are off-limits, but visitors with spotting scopes will find the nest visible from Wildfowl Lane.

White-tailed deer and ring-necked pheasants are abundant and may be encountered just about anywhere, save the open waters. The deer population has exceeded the entire valley's carrying capacity by as much as 20 percent. In the early mornings, deer and pheasants move into crop fields and open areas to feed; the dazzling rooster pheasants scurry across gravel roads or lurk just off the shoulder of the road. Raptors such as the northern harrier, American kestrel, and, occasionally, a golden eagle work the open areas for mice, voles, and other prey.

ACTIVITIES

■ **CAMPING:** While no camping is allowed on Lee Metcalf NWR, there are splendid camping opportunities 5 miles away in Bitterroot National Forest to the west and south, and in the Sapphire Mountains to the east.

■ **SWIMMING:** There is no swimming permitted within refuge boundaries. The Bitterroot River, on the refuge's western boundary, runs clear and cold and may be reached at public-access points along US 93. Relatively tame by late summer, the Bitterroot in all seasons remains swift and deep in places; swimming and boating are unthinkable during spring runoff.

■ **WILDLIFE OBSERVATION:** Early mornings and dusk, year-round, are prime hours for encounters with more elusive wildlife. Otters, beaver, mink, and deer are most active at these times and may be seen by patient viewers on all but the coldest days of winter. Viewing of migratory songbirds begins in late April and peaks in mid- to late May; resident songbirds and woodpeckers are best seen early mornings between April and July. Migrating waterfowl and shorebirds arrive in late March, with peak migration in mid-April. Fall migration for songbirds peaks in mid-September; waterfowl and shorebirds follow, with best viewing mid-October through mid-November. A tour on Wildfowl Lane is your best bet for almost all of these sightings.

■ **PHOTOGRAPHY:** Early summer in the Bitterroot Valley is a photographer's dream made real. In the riverside forest, serviceberry and wild roses and dogwood bloom; the canopy emerges emerald green, and surrounding ranchlands are lush with new grass and gamboling calves. The Bitterroot Mountains retain a brilliant white crown of snowpack against the blue skies. Scenes such as this may be captured along Wildfowl Lane; for a more panoramic view, walk or drive east off the refuge toward Eastside Highway.

■ **HIKES AND WALKS:** Anyone driving Wildfowl Lane will be going very slowly; walking the road is a fine way to explore Metcalf's marshes, ponds, and scattered uplands and croplands. The interconnecting loop trails of the Bitterroot Recreation Area offer the best experience of the forest, river, and associated wildlife and plantlife in this immediate area.

■ **SEASONAL EVENTS:** April: Welcome Back Waterfowl Day, annually in early April.

May: Migration Mania Festival, annually on a Saturday in mid-May, during peak songbird migration. Day-long event featuring exhibits, activities, workshops, music, and bird walks. Speakers discuss the region's avian ecology. Fun and informative for adults and children. Same day: Federal Junior Duck Stamp awards. Lee Metcalf NWR is Montana's point of contact for this annual "Conservation through the Arts" program.

June: Kids Fishing Clinic.

HUNTING AND FISHING
Hunting is permitted for waterfowl (**ducks**, **Canada geese**, **coots**) and only bowhunting is allowed for taking **white-tailed deer**.

Fishing Is permitted in the Bitterroot Recreation Area, with access to the Bitterroot River and its cold-water fishery of **cutthroat**, **brown**, and **rainbow trout**.

■ **PUBLICATIONS:** General brochure; bird list; reptiles list; wildflowers list; hunting information.

Medicine Lake NWR
Medicine Lake, Montana

Mixed grass and shortgrass prairie, Medicine Lake NWR

Here the land is gentle and the wind is forever. Indeed, the climate can be down-right unfriendly around these parts. Everything else, however, about 31,457-acre Medicine Lake NWR is easy, except perhaps getting here, though that's half the fun. Those who make the trek (between 10,000 and 11,000 visitors a year) are rewarded with untrammeled reaches of prairie—including a spectacular wildflower display—and a prolific community of wildlife, most notably birds. Medicine Lake alone is a wondrous piece of glacial work, a wind-ruffled inland sea of 8,700 acres.

HISTORY

For hundreds of years these rolling prairielands were summer pasture for immense bison herds. Plains Indian tribes, such as the Assiniboine, used the pre-sent-day refuge as a gathering site for seasonal hunts. Reminders of this era are scattered about refuge grounds—stone rings mark tipi, or ceremonial sites, and a careful observer may see a few old bison bones.

The refuge was established in 1935 and hosted a Civilian Conservation Corps (CCC) detail two years later. Congress in 1976 designated 11,360 acres here as the Medicine Lake Wilderness Area; the figure is a bit deceiving, as nearly 8,000 of those acres consist of water and marsh.

GETTING THERE

From the south: At the town of Glendive, MT, on I-94, drive north 162 mi. on MT 16, turning right (east) at North Shore Rd., 1 mi. south of the town of Med-icine Lake; continue 2.5 mi. on this gravel route to the refuge office on right. From the east: At the town of Williston, ND, travel west on US 2 for 41 mi., turning right (north) onto MT 16 at the town of Culbertson; continue 11 mi., turning right (east) at North Shore Rd., 1 mi. south of the town of Medicine

Lake; continue 2.5 mi. on this gravel route to the refuge office on right. From the west: At the town of Wolf Point, MT, on US 2, travel east for 55 mi., turning left (north) onto MT 16 at the town of Culbertson; follow directions above.

■ **SEASON:** Open year-round.

■ **HOURS:** Refuge open daylight hours; refuge headquarters, with exhibits of artifacts and specimen counts, is open weekdays, 7 a.m.–3:30 p.m. Visitors arriving when offices are closed will find printed materials and maps at five refuge kiosks near all entrance roads.

■ **FEES:** None.

■ **ADDRESS:** 223 No. Shore Rd., Medicine Lake, MT 59247-9600

■ **TELEPHONE:** 406/789-2305

TOURING MEDICINE LAKE

■ **BY AUTOMOBILE:** A 14-mile self-guided auto-tour route encircling portions of Medicine Lake is open year-round, unless impassable due to wet weather. A portion of the tour route closes during fall hunts, beginning in September.

■ **BY FOOT:** The refuge offers exceptional opportunities for hiking. Walking is permitted year-round on refuge roads, including the auto-tour route and refuge patrol roads. There are no designated trails, but unimproved paths are present; one such trail begins near Stop 7 of the auto-tour route and encircles the Deep Lake Unit for a total distance of about 4 miles. Cross-country travel in the Medicine Lake Wilderness Area and other areas is permitted year-round, though some restrictions apply during the fall hunting season. The Homestead Unit is closed to public access. Check at refuge headquarters for more information.

■ **BY BICYCLE:** Biking is permitted year-round on refuge roads only.

■ **BY CANOE, KAYAK, OR BOAT:** Canoes and nonmotorized rowboats are permitted. Caution: Strong winds can descend suddenly on this immense lake. Refuge officials suggest staying close to shore. No public access is permitted on the islands.

WHAT TO SEE

■ **LANDSCAPE AND CLIMATE** Shallow, sprawling Medicine Lake and its surrounding plains testify to a long-ago collision involving glaciers and the

Wetlands, Medicine Lake NWR

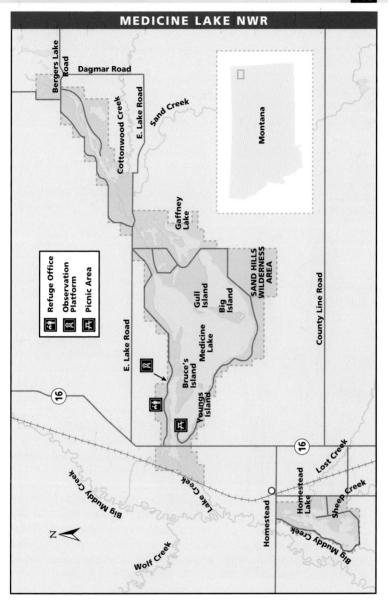

MEDICINE LAKE NWR

Bergers Lake Road

Dagmar Road

Cottonwood Creek

E. Lake Road

Sand Creek

Montana

Gaffney Lake

SAND HILLS WILDERNESS AREA

Refuge Office

Observation Platform

Picnic Area

E. Lake Road

County Line Road

Gull Island

Big Island

Medicine Lake

Bruce's Island

Youngs Island

16

16

Lost Creek

Big Muddy Creek

Lake Creek

Homestead Lake

Sheep Creek

Homestead

Big Muddy Creek

N

Wolf Creek

nation's longest river. Prior to the last Ice Age, the Missouri River flowed north to Hudson Bay, passing through today's refuge. Encroaching ice sheets from Canada blocked its path, forcing the river some 30 miles south and causing it to flow in an easterly direction. Medicine Lake is a remnant of the ancient riverbed, which today lies buried beneath more than 200 feet of glacial gravel.

The sandhills area, on the southeast side of Medicine Lake, is another unusual feature here. A severe drought 6,000 years ago converted the area to desert; north winds delivered sand and dust from the lakebed to the south shore, forming the gentle, vegetated dunes seen here today.

The climate, though variable, is often unforgiving. Winds of 40 to 50 mph are not uncommon. Annual precipitation averages 14 inches, with the majority of it falling as rain in May and June. Following this wet period, the area dries out through summer, with lightning-caused wildfires a possibility in August and September. Spells of extreme cold from Arctic fronts are typical in winter; snowfall is light, averaging about 30 inches.

■ PLANT LIFE AND HABITATS

Wetlands The refuge's 13,000 acres of wetlands begin with seasonal and temporary "potholes" in grassland areas; the potholes hold water from a few weeks to a month or so. Medicine Lake, though vast, is shallow, with depths ranging from 4 to 14 feet and varying, sometimes greatly, by season. Its water sources are seasonal, including Lake Creek, flowing from North Dakota; Sand and Cottonwood creeks, from the east; and a man-made canal delivering water from the west at Big Muddy Creek. Water depths limit emergent vegetation to the lake's outer fringes, though the western end features more extensive marsh. Its waters are fairly alkaline and support a wealth of fairy shrimp; sago pondweed, a waterfowl delicacy, is prolific.

Alkalinity varies in other refuge waters: Katy's Lake is extremely alkaline, while Homestead, Deep Lake, and Lakes 11 and 12 are freshwater. Hardstem bulrush and cattail dominate a thriving marsh complex in these and many other areas. Canals and water-control structures allow for some manipulation of marsh water levels. Also present are expanses of wet meadows, with sedges, rushes, foxtail barley, and western wheatgrass.

Grasslands Located in the transition zone between mixed-grass and short-grass prairie, these undisturbed 14,000 acres feature grasses such as needle-and-thread, June grass, and blue grama. Wildflowers are plentiful, and when rainfall and other factors are ideal, the show begins in early spring and lasts through early fall. Purple

Coneflower

and yellow coneflower, pasqueflowers, and Indian paintbrush intermingle with silver sage and other flower species. Crested wheatgrass is the primary exotic here, a variety with minimal wildlife value that competes with native grasses. It is the first to green up in spring, at which time the refuge hammers at it with a combination of prescribed burning and short-duration grazing, setting it back for the year before native grasses have begun to grow. Prairie rose and western snowberry are representative woody species.

Other habitats The Sandhills features surprises—among them, three varieties of cacti, plus grasses such as prairie sand reed and shrubs such as chokecherry. A complete survey of Sandhills plant life is soon to be completed, and refuge staff are learning about other species, some possibly rare, that live here.

Three Islands in Medicine Lake have mixed-grass prairie, though Young's Island is dominated by greasewood, a salt-tolerant shrub with smooth, gray bark and fleshy leaves. It's popular with Canada geese: Just 17 acres in size, the island hosts as many as 70 goose nests.

About 4,000 acres of historic crop-land—land that had been farmed for many years—are planted in dense nesting cover for waterfowl, with alfalfa and wheatgrasses the dominant plants. Every 10 to 15 years, this land is tilled and cropped to reestablish cover, which deteriorates over time.

■ ANIMAL LIFE

Birds A whole lot of breeding goes on here. Medicine Lake hosts the state's largest nesting colony of American white pelicans, and 80 percent of Montana's threatened piping plovers in and around the refuge. There are large rookeries of both great blue heron and black-crowned night-heron, double-crested cormorant, Forster's tern, and common tern. Add four species of nesting grebe and 12 nesting duck species, and a visitor

Prairie falcon

in midsummer is assured of seeing all manner of gawky, fuzzy young. Shorebirds—willet, American avocet, common snipe, marbled godwit—are abundant in summer, with many more appearing during spring and fall migrations.

This is raptor country, too, and you have good chances of seeing many species here. The ferruginous and Swainson's hawk nest on-site; prairie falcons nest nearby, as do golden eagles, which are distinguished from bald by their brown color and golden nape. Peregrine falcons are seen every year. Short-eared owls occur in sizable numbers; burrowing owls are present. In late fall and early spring, as many as 100 bald eagles at a time are seen along the lakeshore.

The refuge's expansive prairie hosts several uncommon songbirds. Baird's and grasshopper sparrows, chestnut-collared longspur, bobolink, and Sprague's pipit thrive here; LeConte's and sharp-tailed sparrows are uncommon. Other songsters are everywhere: horned lark, kingbirds, lark bunting, western meadowlark, and yellow-headed blackbird. Uncommon nesting species such as the American redstart and yellow-breasted chat are found here. A thriving community of sharp-tailed grouse perform their lovely courtship rituals in April and May. Gray partridge and ring-necked pheasant are common.

Fall migration brings an enormous buildup of waterfowl, along with a high diversity of shorebirds. Sandhill cranes, which stop here during both migratory trips, remain longer in fall, with flocks of 5,000 present. Tundra swans, an occasional trumpeter swan, and ducks galore—ruddy duck, bufflehead, American wigeon, mergansers, mallard, blue-winged and green-winged teal—visit in spring and fall, as do large numbers of white-fronted and Canada geese.

Mammals It's hard not to see white-tailed deer in the prairie and planted fields. Mule deer occur in limited numbers, as do pronghorn, those lovely speedsters of open country. Proghorn are a species unto themselves—they are neither deer nor antelope, and their horns are just that: horns, not antlers. Where there are nesting birds, expect to find coyote and red fox, and both are on the prowl here early and late in the day. Burrowing rodents include the Richardson's and thirteen-lined ground squirrels. Water-dependent species here include the beaver, muskrat, mink, and several varieties of shrew. The long-tailed and least weasels are residents, along with the highly adaptable porcupine.

Reptiles and amphibians The refuge is thick with tiger salamanders, another important food item for birds, and visitors who inspect the shady, cool areas around refuge headquarters will almost surely see a few. Also present is the bull snake, a very large, beautifully marked species that is nonvenomous, though it coils and strikes much like a rattlesnake when threatened. No rattlesnakes live here. This is the only site in Montana known to support the smooth green snake, a very elusive creature not likely to be seen. The Plains garter snake and ribbon snake have also been recorded.

A surprisingly rich array of frogs and toads enliven spring and summer nights at Medicine Lake—Woodhouse's toad, cricket frog, and chorus frog are the common species, with a few northern leopard frogs present.

Fish Medicine Lake's fishery is short on sport species—only the northern pike is maintained through stocking. Fish pursued by the many herons, pelicans, and cormorants here are the fathead minnow, white sucker, and carp.

ACTIVITIES

■ **CAMPING:** Camping is not permitted; a list of area campgrounds is available from refuge headquarters.

■ **SWIMMING:** No swimming is allowed on the refuge; the main lake lies in a federally protected Wilderness Area.

■ **WILDLIFE OBSERVATION:** Bridgerman Point is the place to visit for great viewing of colonial birds nesting on islands. All-weather binoculars mounted on a viewing platform are here, and visitors will see pelicans, night-herons, and many other birds raising their young. The May–June courtship displays of western grebes are outlandishly beautiful—these water birds literally run atop the water in unison. MT 16, cutting through the refuge, has several turnouts for vehicles, prime vantage points for seeing the grebes. A few whooping cranes visit Medicine Lake each year during spring or fall migration.

> **HUNTING AND FISHING** Hunting for upland birds (**sharp-tailed grouse**, **ring-necked pheasant**, **gray partridge**) is permitted Sept. to Dec. **Waterfowl** hunting seasons runs from Oct. to Jan. **White-tailed deer** can be hunted from late Oct. to late Nov. Fishing is permitted in designated areas on Medicine and three other refuge lakes; seasons and access vary for each, though limited nonmotorized boat and bank access is available. **Walleye** and **northern pike** are the sought-after species.

■ **PHOTOGRAPHY:** Photographers will find much to capture on film—waterfowl, pelicans and herons with young, and dancing sharp-tailed grouse in April and May. A 100-foot-high observation tower at refuge headquarters allows for panoramas; beautiful sunrises and sunsets color Medicine Lake.

■ **HIKES AND WALKS:** The viewing platform at Bridgerman Point is adjacent to a large tract of native prairie. Take a cross-country stroll here amid vast skies, seasonal wildflowers, and birdsong. A walk up onto the Tipi Hills is another good hike, with a stunning overview of the refuge and the chance to see many scattered ceremonial stone rings.

■ **SEASONAL EVENTS:** Oct.: National Wildlife Refuge Week

■ **PUBLICATIONS:** Bird, wildflower, and mammal lists; refuge brochure.

National Bison Range
Moiese, Montana

Bison mother and calf, National Bison Range

The American bison has survived near extermination and is well reestablished in its modern incarnation as a tourist attraction at parks and refuges throughout the country. The wild herd of 350 to 500 bison that grazes the grasslands of the National Bison Range (NBR) need only stand in place—each weighing some 2,000 pounds, with a great humped back, stout, powerful legs, and fetching, woolly beard—to inspire people and even give them a sense of the large, great promise of this country, of free-roaming herds and a wide-open landscape.

The refuge is located in the Mission Valley within the Flathead Indian Reservation. The scenery alone would make for a memorable visit, but the Bison Range, highly accessible and visitor-friendly, offers much more, especially for families. The Visitor Center is sleek and modern, filled with exhibits, books, videos, and helpful staff, all geared toward enriching the public's appreciation for the landscape and wildlife here.

There is, indeed, much to appreciate. The Palouse Prairie in midsummer is alive with wildflowers and a great variety of birds. Along with bison, visitors may encounter several other charismatic Rocky Mountain mammals—elk, mule and white-tailed deer, mountain goats, bighorn sheep, and pronghorn antelope. NBR continues to grow in popularity, and summertime traffic along the tour routes is often heavy and slow in July and August.

HISTORY

When a Pend d' Oreille (pronounced pon-der-ray) Indian named Walking Coyote returned home to this valley with five orphaned bison calves, it was 1873: the American Frontier was closing, and of the Great Plains bison herds that had numbered perhaps 60 million, about 1,000 animals survived. Walking Coyote's orphans became a herd of 13, which he later sold to two ranchers. In the years that followed, their herds would become the largest in the nation.

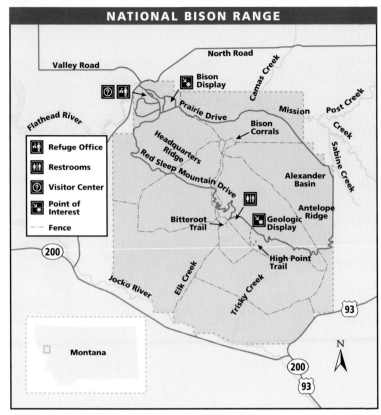

NATIONAL BISON RANGE

When one of the ranchers later sold his herd to Canada, public protest spurred conservationists to pressure Washington. In 1908, President Theodore Roosevelt authorized the purchase of some 18,000 acres from the Confederated Tribes of the Flathead, Kootenai, and Pend d' Oreille Indians for a permanent "national bison range," the first-ever land purchase for wildlife by the federal government.

NBR has gone on to play an important role in bison recovery, each year culling and selling off a number of animals to augment private and public herds throughout the country. North America's bison population today is estimated at 200,000, including a growing percentage raised for food. One suspects Walking Coyote would be pleased.

GETTING THERE

From Missoula, travel north on US 93 for 37 mi. to the town of Ravalli; turn west onto MT 200 and drive 6 mi. to Dixon, turning north onto Secondary Rte. 212, following it 4 mi. to refuge entrance. From Polson, drive south on US 93 through Ronan; 4 mi. south of town, turn right onto Secondary Rte. 212 and continue 13 mi. to refuge entrance.

■ **SEASON:** Visitor Center and refuge offices open year-round.

■ **HOURS:** Main gates open 7 a.m. and close at dark throughout the year. Visitor Center open daily during summer season (mid-May to late Oct.), weekdays rest of year (closed weekends and holidays).

■ **FEES:** $4 per vehicle; federal-fee area Golden Passes and Federal Duck Stamps accepted.
■ **ADDRESS:** 132 Bison Range Rd., Moiese, MT 59824
■ **TELEPHONE:** 406/644-2211

TOURING THE NATIONAL BISON RANGE

■ **BY AUTOMOBILE:** Three tour routes are the primary means of access at NBR. The Prairie Dr./West Loop is a 5-mile gravel road open year-round and accessible to vehicles with trailers and large RVs; the Red Sleep Mountain Dr. is a 19-mile, one-way gravel road open mid-May to late October—no vehicles longer than 30 feet are permitted; the Winter Dr. is a 10-mile gravel road open late October to mid-May.

■ **BY FOOT:** Hiking is permitted only on designated footpaths, which include the wheelchair-accessible Nature Trail (1.0 mi.) near the picnic area; the Bitterroot Trail, about 0.5 mi. long; and the mile-long High Point Trail.

■ **BY BICYCLE AND MOTORCYCLE:** All bikes are restricted to paved drives around the Visitor Center and bison display pasture and are not permitted on any of the graveled tour routes. Too much traffic.

■ **BY CANOE, KAYAK, OR BOAT:** There is no boating on the refuge.

WHAT TO SEE

■ **LANDSCAPE AND CLIMATE** The Mission Valley is a part of the Columbia River Basin; waters on the refuge flow from Mission Creek and the Jocko River into the Flathead River, and then into the Clark Fork, which flows into Lake Pend Oreille in Idaho. The Pend Oreille River exits the lake and flows north into British Columbia, where it meets the mighty Columbia River just north of the Canadian border. The site encompasses one modest, rolling mountain. Refuge headquarters is at 2,582 feet with elevations reaching to 4,885 feet along High Point Trail a few miles to the south. Due east approximately 15 mi., the bladelike peaks of the Mission Mountains climb to 9,000 feet. The Missions trend north-south, as the eastern boundary of the Flathead Valley, the natural centerpiece of

Palouse Prairie, National Bison Range

which is 200-square-mile Flathead Lake. Formed by an immense block of glacial ice, this is the largest natural freshwater lake west of the Mississippi.

Flathead Lake is large enough to influence climate; along its shores, where temperatures remain milder in winter and precipitation is more dependable, a booming agricultural industry turns out cherries, blueberries, apples, and even some respectable wines from area vineyards. On the Bison Range, however, the lake has little or no effect, and the yearly precipitation total of 13 inches is quite similar to that of the semiarid region east of the Continental Divide.

■ PLANT LIFE AND HABITATS

Open waters Mission Creek and the Jocko River meander along the north and south boundaries of the Bison Range. Both are clear and cold, fed by snowmelt, and support a variety of fish both native and introduced. Native species in the Jocko include the threatened bull trout, as well as the native westslope cutthroat trout and whitefish; rainbow and brown trout inhabit both the creek and the river. A series of ponds along Mission Creek features sedges, horsetail, cattail, spike rushes, bulrush, and pondweed.

Shooting star, National Bison Range

Grasslands The dominant plant community on NBR is native Palouse Prairie. Widespread across western Montana and the drier reaches of the Pacific Northwest prior to settlement, this grassland biome is extremely rare today. Along with grasses such as Idaho fescue, bluebunch wheatgrass and rough fescue is a wide array of forbs, or broad-leafed plants—meaning wildflowers. Spring beauty, larkspur, cinquefoils, milk vetch, shooting star, harebell, forget-me-not, lupine, balsamroot and penstemon represent only a small sampling; more than 240 wildflower species in all have been recorded here. NBR does yearly battle with exotic plants, employing a combination of chemical spraying and biological control to mitigate the likes of St.-John's-wort, toadflax, spotted knapweed, and Canada thistle; efforts to control purple loosestrife have been declared a success—the pesky nonnative never really got a foothold in the valley because of early identification, hand-pulling (both by individuals and during scheduled group pulls), and through the release of biocontrol insects.

Forests Less than one-quarter of refuge lands support a montane forest , with ponderosa pine and Douglas fir the dominant tree species; ponderosas favor south-facing, or warmer, exposed sites, while the firs occupy cooler north-facing drainages and other sites with more moisture and shade. Scattered stands of aspen and Rocky Mountain maple are part of the mix as well, especially in cooler, wetter areas. Forested areas provide important shelter for elk, deer, and black bear, as well as nesting sites for a variety of birds.

Along Mission Creek and the Jocko River is a rich and quite diverse bottom-land deciduous forest. The tallest members are narrowleaf and black cottonwood, along with aspen, Rocky Mountain juniper, black hawthorn, thinleaf and mountain alder, serviceberry, willow and water birch. An assortment of shrub species is also present, among them red-osier dogwood, woods rose, and chokecherry.

■ ANIMAL LIFE

Birds Birdlife varies from grassland songbirds and raptors to a diversity of species in streamside willow thickets and deciduous forests. Six swallow species are all common here, including northern rough-winged and tree swallows; their cousins, the black and Vaux's swifts, are seen occasionally—all favor Mission Creek's open waters and associated ponds. In willows and cottonwoods along the creek and Jocko River are MacGillivray's warblers, common yellowthroats, red-eyed vireos and the spotted towhee. Common grassland songsters at NBR include the mountain blue-bird, grasshopper and sparrow, and the occasional rosy finch.

Mountain bluebird

Golden eagles nest on the refuge and are frequently seen aloft. Sharp-shinned and Cooper's hawks are sighted occasionally in cottonwood and coniferous forests; the rough-legged hawk, American kestrel, and northern harrier are all common, but the prairie falcon, bald eagle, and northern goshawk are seen only occasionally.

Mammals The executive order creating NBR included construction of a "good and substantial fence," and substantial it is; nothing less would prevent the bison, North America's largest land animal, from going exactly where it wanted to go. Though all of the large hoofed mammals here are captive, 18,500 acres is a sizable piece of land—bison, along with elk, mule deer, pronghorn antelope, mountain goats, and bighorn sheep, are often on the move, occupying different areas of the site at different times of day and through the seasons. Sometimes they are easily seen, sometimes not. Because most viewing is along roadsides, visitors are allowed to slow and stop for photos or extended looks, but walking away from parked vehicles is forbidden, except when parking to hike a designated foot trail.

Small mammals include the yellow-bellied marmot, with its signature high-pitched whistle. The marmot may be seen in higher elevations with rocky outcrops and along Mission Creek. Forested areas are home to the yellow-pine chipmunk, red squirrel, and porcupine. A variety of grassland rodents, including the Columbian ground squirrel and three vole species, are the prey base for badgers and coyotes. Streamside forests of Mission Creek and the Jocko River are the haunts for the occasional beaver; white-tailed deer, muskrat, and mink may be encountered here, too.

Reptiles and amphibians Amphibian life includes the tiger, long-toed, and Coeur D'Alene salamanders; the Pacific tree frog, western toad, and spotted frog inhabit pond and stream edges. Grasslands and rocky areas support prairie rattlesnakes, the common and western garter snakes, and the western yellow-bellied racer.

ACTIVITIES

■ **CAMPING:** No camping on refuge property.

■ **SWIMMING:** No swimming.

■ **WILDLIFE OBSERVATION:** The interaction of grazing animals with a grassland constitutes one of nature's great achievements, and NBR is a perfect place to see this relationship in action. A 2,000-pound bison or 700-pound elk needs a lot of food every day. Add a herd of mule deer and another of pronghorn, and the question arises—with such an abundance of large animals chomping away at the prairie, how is it that any plants are left standing at all? The grasslands at NBR are thriving; the animals are doing things right.

One factor involves the digestive system of each species. Bison and elk are "primary grazers," which means their larger stomachs can accommodate tougher, more mature plants — stems, leaves, and all. Deer and antelope are "secondary grazers"; they focus on newer, more tender grasses and emerging growth. In a natural system, bison and elk clear the way for deer and pronghorn.

HOOVES AND DUST It's the event many refuge workers wait all year for. The pickup truck is traded for a favorite horse. It's time to round up the bison.

The annual culling of the NBR herd is an old-time western roundup with bison standing in for cattle, a far wilder and woollier proposition. For those who have yet to witness an American bison do anything other than stand motionless, a visit to the roundup will dispel any ideas that this is a lethargic or clumsy beast—or a mild-tempered one.

NBR's grasslands can support a herd of 370 bison through the winter, and for 90 years now the herd has undergone a fall culling, in which the entire herd is rounded up and moved first into a steep ravine, and then, over two days, "cut" by wranglers into groups of two dozen and pushed downslope into a corral. Here the animals are vaccinated, branded, and weighed. About 100 bison are donated or sold through a sealed bid to private landowners, Indian tribes, bison researchers, or other wildlife refuges. The remainder return to their home on the range.

The two-day event draws thousands of spectators; they line the fences and catwalks above chutes and holding pens, marveling at the speed and power of these animals—which can reach speeds of 35 mph—and the skills of the wranglers who drive them in, often at breakneck speed, amidst plumes of dust and drumming hooves.

Grazing actually has an important regenerative effect on grasses and wildflowers. Prairies have been grazed for so many thousands of years that plants not only cope with grazing—they thrive on it. Grazing is like mowing the lawn: Taller leaves are clipped, the stem is unharmed, and the grass immediately begins to send out new growth. The effect on forbs (wildflowers) is akin to pinching back a cultivated flower—the plant's root system becomes more vigorous, its regrowth often fuller.

Animals have food preferences, too: Each species favors certain varieties of grasses and flowers, and at certain times of the year. This is why diversity is so essential for healthy grasslands and grazers; if a handful of native species are lost, those that remain become vulnerable to overgrazing and may not be able to reproduce, throwing the whole system out of balance.

■ **PHOTOGRAPHY:** Bison are very dark brown and sometimes black. To capture their features on film, use slightly longer exposure times or you may get images of little more than hulking silouhettes. Bison photographs taken in full sun turn out best.

Panoramic images of wildflower-colored meadows with rich green grasses and the snow-capped Mission Mountains are possible from High Point Trail and along Red Sleep Drive; mid- to late evenings in June and early July are the best times. Buckskin-colored bison calves appear mid-April through May; songbird activity commences in mid-May and continues through early August.

American bison, National Bison Range

■ **HIKES AND WALKS:** While not the featured means of exploring NBR, a few pleasant walks are possible, each allowing some views of a distinctly different natural area. The Nature Trail is a paved footpath that crosses a wheelchair-accessible fishing platform and then circles the largest of three ponds along Mission Creek. A good area to hear or see songbirds, check the pond also for waterfowl and the occasional shorebird. An unimproved trail splits off from the paved route just beyond the parking area, goes by a smaller pond and follows Mission Creek for about 0.66 miles upstream. On a hot day this is a cool, shady place, and the creek is a beauty. The Bitterroot and High Point trails have trailheads at the top of Red Sleep Drive Both trails offer excellent views of the gorgeous adjoining lands and allow exploration of the montane forest. These are good places to watch for elk, mule deer, and mountain goats. A geologic display, located at the pullout along the tour route at the High Point trailhead, interprets the glacial history of the region.

HUNTING AND FISHING
There is no hunting on the refuge.

You can fish for **brown trout, rainbow trout**, and **whitefish** from May to mid-Nov.

■ **SEASONAL EVENTS:** May: International Migratory Bird Day, second weekend, with walks and speakers; October: The most celebrated event here is the annual bison roundup, attracting many visitors (see sidebar, p. 108).

■ **PUBLICATIONS:** Literature on the annual bison roundup; interpretive materials on NBR's plant and animal communities; bird and mammal checklists; refuge brochure.

Red Rock Lakes NWR
Lima, Montana

Red Rock Lakes NWR

The only sounds here are wild sounds. The *kaaroooo* of a pair of sandhill cranes rising into flight, the chatter of ducks, whirring wings, a coyote's yap. The cry of a Swainson's hawk. Morning stillness broken by the deep, resonant note of a trumpeter swan. The views to the north seem endless, open lands of sagebrush and sweet clover rolling on and on, ending in sky. To the south is a great wall of rock: the Centennial Mountains, high peaks mottled with snow, black-green forests unrolling over the steep slopes. Rare and remarkable creatures—the wolverine, lynx, grizzly bear, peregrine falcon—make these mountains their home. At this second turn of a century, it's hard to believe that virtually all the valleys in the West were once as unshackled and free as the Centennial remains today.

HISTORY

Much of what is Red Rock was homesteaded at the turn of the last century. The Centennial Valley is so named because livestock were brought in in 1876, the nation's centennial. By the early 1930s, both its human inhabitants and one of North America's great birds, the trumpeter swan, were facing hard times. Hunted, captured, or killed for sale to zoos and museums, the swan species was in serious decline. Meanwhile, an unsettled economy and a difficult climate combined to drive many settlers out of the valley. Red Rock refuge was established in 1935 largely to save the trumpeter swan. Red Rock would go on to play a pivotal role in one of the nation's first conservation triumphs. The trumpeter swan population hovered near 69 birds in 1932; today the refuge hosts a breeding population of about 500, largest in the lower 48. The 44,963-acre refuge has since been designated a National Natural Landmark; of that acreage, 32,350 acres are designated Wilderness Area land.

GETTING THERE

From the west: Exit I-15 at Monida, Montana, and drive 28 mi. east on Red Rock

Pass Rd. to refuge headquarters in Lakeview. The east entrance is the best choice for visitors coming from West Yellowstone, Montana. Follow US 20 west for 12 mi. to the junction with MT 87. Travel north for 5 mi., turning west at refuge sign onto Red Rock Pass Rd.; continue 30 mi. to refuge boundary. Don't leave the pavement without a full tank of gas; a round-trip will average about 100 mi., including refuge visit, and no fuel is available in the Centennial Valley. The nearest places to buy gas are in Lima, Montana; Dubois, Idaho; and the Island Park or Henry's Lake area in Idaho.

- **SEASON:** Open year-round, 7:30 a.m.–4 p.m., Mon.–Fri.
- **HOURS:** Dawn to dusk.
- **FEES:** None.
- **ADDRESS:** Monida Star Rte., Box 15, Lima, MT 59739
- **TELEPHONE:** 406/276-3536

TOURING RED ROCK LAKES

- **BY AUTOMOBILE:** Red Rock Pass Rd., North Side Rd., and Elk Lake Rd. are open to vehicles year-round, weather permitting—all are good places for viewing antelope, fox, coyotes, badgers, moose, and birds. Lower Lake Rd. is open May 15 through mid-November; Culver Rd. open July 15 through September 30; Idlewild Trail open September 1 through December 1. Snowmobiles and ATVs are allowed on through-roads only. None of the roads are official auto-tour roads.
- **BY FOOT:** In keeping with its wilderness spirit, there are no designated or maintained trails at Red Rock, visitors are definitely encouraged to explore on their own and follow numerous game trails or walk cross-country. The splendid Continental Divide Trail is atop the Centennial Mountains and can be accessed from the refuge through primitive routes.
- **BY BICYCLE:** Biking is a productive way to explore from midsummer through late fall. Bicycles are limited to refuge roads, but this is by no means a setback. Vehicular traffic is virtually nonexistent, making all roads ideal. Terrain is level, although many roads feature coarse gravel, mud, and ruts.
- **BY CANOE, KAYAK, OR BOAT:** Red Rock's namesake lakes provide unparalleled opportunities for wildlife observation via canoe, kayak, rowboat, or other nonmotorized crafts. Boating is permitted on the Upper Lake from July 15 to freeze-up; Lower Lake from September 1 to freeze-up. Strong winds are not uncommon, and the lakes catch all of it. Beautiful Red Rock Creek is also a possibility for canoeists or kayakers from July 15 through freeze-up.

WHAT TO SEE

- **LANDSCAPE AND CLIMATE** The Centennial is a high-elevation valley, high even by Rockies standards, at 6,600 feet. From this "low point," the landscape rises gently 200 to 400 feet to the north, while to the south it ascends dramatically to 10,000 feet along the Centennial Mountains, one of the few North American ranges situated on an east-west axis. The Centennials lie along the Continental Divide; just east of the refuge, atop the Divide on the Montana–Idaho border, tiny Hellroaring Creek constitutes the true headwaters of the Missouri River.

Red Rock forms the western edge of an immense core of wildlands known as the Greater Yellowstone Ecosystem. Encompassing an area the size of Switzerland—in Idaho, Montana, and Wyoming—this biologically intact region maintains every major species of wildlife encountered by the first explorers. Of those 18 million acres, 15 million are in public hands, including Yellowstone and Grand Teton national parks and the National Elk Refuge (see separate entry).

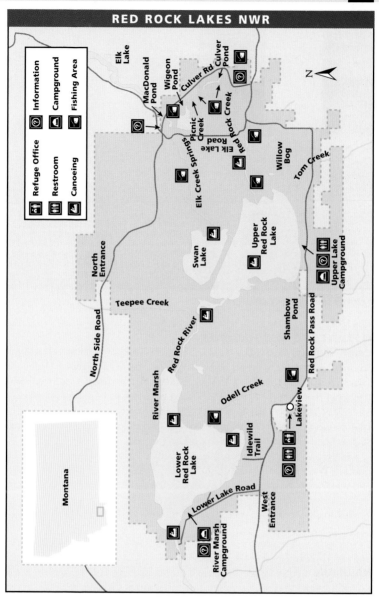

RED ROCK LAKES NWR

Winters are lengthy with prolific snowfall, especially along the Continental Divide. Total annual precipitation (rain and melted snow) at the refuge averages 18.7 inches. The average high temperature at Red Rock in 1998 was 49.1 degrees, the average low, 24.1. Snow is possible any month of the year; the first hard freeze arrives in August.

Snowmelt nourishes the refuge's five major streams, which in turn recharge lakes, marshes, fens, and wet meadows. Water flows east to west, entering Upper Red Rock Lake and passing into the Lower Lake via River Marsh, a shallow, meandering stream. The Lower Lake outlet is dammed, providing a minor degree of control over water levels. Below the outlet, the Red Rock River flows to the west.

Sunflowers and phlox, Red Rock Lakes NWR

■ PLANT LIFE AND HABITATS

Open waters Red Rock's lakes and ponds encompass 9,000 acres; add five streams, and the role of aquatic habitat expands again. The sprawling Upper and Lower lakes appear fathomless. In truth, they're disappearing. Both are shallow— the Upper lake is 4 to 6 feet deep, the Lower 2 to 3 feet—and eutrophication is well under way. The Lower lake has already advanced to marsh and fen in places. The lakes' rich, mucky bottoms are a boon to waterfowl, supporting aquatic vegetation such as pondweed, duckweed, milfoil, and muskgrass.

On the east side, Culver and Wigeon ponds serve as home to the rare arctic grayling. Water clarity borders on surreal; it's possible to count every stone, large and small, cobbling the bottom. Fish remain largely invisible, given away only by the occasional flash or dimpling of the surface.

Red Rock, Odell, Elk Springs, and Tom creeks harbor native westslope cut- throat trout, a species in steady decline, as well as willow riparian corridors. Some 14 species of willow grow here, including booth, geyer, bebb, and plainleaf; alder and silverberry are part of the mix as well.

Wetlands Bordering the Upper and Lower lakes, Swan Lake, and the small ponds and sloughs along North Side Road are some of the most naturally diverse and productive wetlands in the nation. All of the following wetland types are extensively represented.

Wet meadows Landscapes of grasses, sedges, and rushes occurring on "subirrigated" ground, wet meadows have water close to the surface, readily avail- able. Important species here are tufted hairgrass, bluejoint, and spike sedge; where alkalinity is high, salt grass, alkali grass, and basin wildrye hold forth.

Marshes Wetter than meadows, marshes have standing water, at least through the growing season. Hardstem bulrush, cattail, beaked and water sedge, and blue- joint reed grass are present. Most of the wetlands immediately adjacent to Red Rock's lakes are marshes.

Fens The fen is a transition community between marsh and bog; water passes into and out of it, like a marsh, but the movement is slow enough so that, like a bog, peat and other organic materials build up. At Red Rock, the dominant plants in the fens resemble species in the marshes. Willow Bog, at the east end of the refuge between Red Rock and Tom creeks, is actually a fen. In some areas, fens also support willows and shrubby cinquefoil.

Sagebrush grasslands Spread over sweeping flats, stream terraces, and rolling hills are sagebrush grasslands. This is a climax community, the end of the successional line. From the point of view of a songbird or pocket gopher, mature sagebrush is an old-growth forest, offering shade, nesting sites, and, on the ground, a lush understory of grasses and wildflowers.

Red Rock's sagebrush grasslands are diverse and thriving. Five sagebrush types are here, including big sagebrush and two subspecies (mountain big, basin big), silver and three-tip, and low and early low sagebrush. A sampling of the many understory grasses includes Idaho fescue, western needlegrass, Baltic rush, and mountain bromegrass. Wildflowers in the understory include lupine, prairie smoke, yarrow, sticky geranium, slender cinquefoil, and gayfeather. Prairie smoke produces reddish-purple flowers whose seeds form feathery styles that float on the wind, resembling puffs of smoke.

Stabilized sandhills The small rolling hills in the north of the refuge are a unique landscape in Montana; only the Medicine Lake Sandhills (see Medicine Lake NWR) are more extensive. These hills are the dried-up and wind-dispersed remains of a prehistoric lakebed, the predecessor to today's waters. Portions of the hills, known as blowouts, are still shifting around, though they do support vegetation. Four plants considered rare in Montana are here; a rare tiger beetle may also be a resident. A rare plant community of thickspike wheatgrass and silverleaf phaceilia survives as well. Big sagebrush and rabbit brush stabilize the porous, sandy soil; understory plants include heath aster and needle-and-thread grass.

Western tanager

Spruce-fir forests South of Red Rock Pass Road, the land ascends the flanks of the Centennial Mountains into mature woodlands of Douglas fir, Englemann spruce, scattered lodgepole pine, and, farther up, fir and limber pine. Prior to settlement the forest was subject to periodic wildfires, which cleared out shrubs, saplings, and dead and downed trees. With fire suppression a reality, the forest is a different place. What it has become—a dense, tangled world—is an increasingly rare place. Timber harvesting, practiced throughout the region, precludes the buildup of all this good stuff, and the species of wildlife that utilize it have declined elsewhere. With this in mind, refuge management has no immediate plans to intervene, except to carefully manage prescribed burns.

Aspen forests Along Red Rock Creek and other drainages and damp sites to the east, and scattered along the base of the mountains, are stands of aspen parkland. Aspen are colonizers, moving into areas disturbed by flood, fire, road-building, and other events. They seldom reproduce by seed, opting instead for cloning themselves through linked root systems. Fire is an important component of aspen reproduction; fire eliminates an overstory of conifers, whose presence would otherwise inhibit the growth of aspens.

■ **ANIMAL LIFE** Red Rock's open waters, wetlands, and wet meadows pulse with life—waterfowl, shorebirds, songbirds, terns and gulls, and mammals large and small.

The most famous resident is the trumpeter swan, North America's largest waterfowl. Six species of grebe also nest here. Ducks are diverse and abundant: teal, ruddy duck, canvasback, and bufflehead are nesters. American white pelicans are often on the wing. Along marsh edges and mudflats are sora, American avocet, and marsh wrens. The black-necked stilt and white-faced ibis are seen occasionally. Marshes host a variety of rodents, such as the muskrat, and Gapper's red-backed mouse.

The riparian thickets of willows and alder lining streams and ditches are a world unto themselves. This is the favored haunt of the refuge's sizable moose population; the Shiras moose is slightly smaller than its New England cousin. The willow flycatcher, common yellowthroat, and Wilson's warbler nest here. River otter, mink, and beavers inhabit all stream areas.

The drier sagbrush grasslands and sandhills are favored by fleet-footed

Red squirrel

pronghorn along with sandhill cranes and numerous small mammals—white-tailed jackrabbit, northern pocket gopher, and Richardson's ground squirrel. A thriving rodent population means a thriving raptor community: The short-eared owl, prairie falcon, and Swainson's hawk are common; ferruginous hawks and merlins are seen less frequently here. True to their names, sage grouse and sage thrashers inhabit the dry lands, as do larks and a full complement of grassland sparrows—savannah, Brewer's, Lincoln's, and several others.

Lynx

The forested mountains shelter rare, remarkable carnivores—the wolverine, lynx, and pine marten—as well as their more easily sighted prey: red squirrels, golden-manteled ground squirrels, and yellow pine chipmunk. Wolves and grizzly bears wander through, rarely sighted. Yellow-bellied marmots and pikas like the high, rocky ridges of the mountains. In fall, herds of elk pass through the valley, migrating north to a winter range; in spring they make the return trip. Mule deer and white-tailed deer are seen more frequently along forest edges.

The forested areas and high ridges feature some notable birds. The area is home to four confirmed breeding pairs of peregrine falcons, which routinely fly from the high cliffs to hunt over the valley. Songbirds such as the western wood peewee, western tanager, and warbling vireo nest in conifers and aspens. Mature, tangled woodlands mean woodpeckers, and they're here, eight species in all, including such notables as the three-toed, black-backed, and Lewis'.

ACTIVITIES

■ **CAMPING:** Two primitive campgrounds are located on the refuge; no fees are charged and no reservations are accepted. River Marsh, on open grasslands at the west end of Lower Red Rock Lake, has toilets and fire rings but no potable water; there is fine birding for water-associated species right at the site. Upper Lake Campground, on the Upper Lake's southern shore, is a bit more exposed to the wind but offers the best access for canoeists and kayakers after July 15, plus toilets, spring water, fire rings, and picnic tables.

■ **SWIMMING:** No swimming is permitted within refuge boundaries.

■ **WILDLIFE OBSERVATION:** Refuge roads and the two campgrounds access all major habitats. A good strategy is to pick one area and stay with it through prime wildlife hours. Park and scan the area before exiting the vehicle. After that, try a pleasant walk down the road or around the campground, as far as the spirit moves. While walking, keep an eye out for footpaths or game trails going off into the landscape. It is permissible to walk anywhere except for areas marked as closed, and trails often lead to something special—a wildflower meadow, a secluded inlet, a shed moose antler (but no collecting is allowed). Spring arrives late in this high valley; from mid-April through May visitors willing to endure rain and mud will see the refuge awakening. It's a noisy, hectic time, as all birdlife returns. This is also the best time—perhaps the only time—to see elk. Wildflowers bloom in June, and in mid-June the mosquitoes come. Mosquitoes here are legendary; even the most tough-skinned visitor will come away impressed. The summer herd of moose, 30 to 35 strong, enters the willow thickets; about 90 percent of all sightings occur in this habitat. By late summer and early fall the mosquitoes are gone or on the wane; mornings and evenings are cool. Canoeing the lakes at this time offers reliable viewing of waterfowl and chances to see water-associated mammals. Raptors are abundant throughout the year, whether soaring or perched on telephone poles and trees along forest edges.

■ **PHOTOGRAPHY:** Panoramas of the Centennial Valley are a constant temptation but seldom achieve the desired results, especially in full sunlight. The Centennial Mountains are backlit through the middle of the day, but good shots can be had during mornings and late afternoons in summer from North Side Road. The Lower Campground is a prime spot for photographing waterfowl (trumpeter swans are reclusive; luck is required), as is the Lower Lake. Ruins of homesites and long-abandoned farm implements dot the sagebrush grasslands to the north.

> **HUNTING AND FISHING** Big-game species include **pronghorn antelope**, **white-tailed** and **mule deer**, **elk**, and **moose** (by permit only). **Waterfowl** hunting is permitted, but there is no upland bird hunting.
>
> Fishing is permitted for **brook**, **rainbow**, and **cutthroat trout** in refuge streams and on some ponds. **Arctic grayling** inhabit some waters and any caught must be released. No fishing in main lakes.

■ **HIKES AND WALKS:** The Upper Campground is a good starting point for an uphill walk into the forests and mountains. From the campground, simply cross the road and pick up a game trail. On the far east end of the refuge, Red Rock Creek is a treat to wander along; terrain is level and open but rough, with numerous grassy flats. Beware of moose in the willows. Culver Road, which crosses the creek just inside the east boundary, is another open, level walk, with opportunities to explore some ponds. But people are allowed to walk anywhere on the refuge and rarely use the road.

■ **SEASONAL EVENTS:** None.

■ **PUBLICATIONS:** General refuge brochure with map; checklists of birds, including the history of the trumpeter swan at Red Rock; one-page handouts on other species.

Bear River Migratory Bird Refuge
Brigham City, Utah

American white pelicans

From its origins in rolling plains, the western landscape progresses toward the elemental. Here on the floor of the Great Basin, the view encompasses one of its most forceful expressions. Bare-faced, deeply chiseled mountains loom above expanses of salt-encrusted desert. In the heat-soaked light, it is difficult to know just where land ends and where the vast primordial sea, the Great Salt Lake, begins. Everything shimmers. Biblical tableaus—Mount Sinai, the desert as wilderness, the Red Sea—are made tangible.

Against all that is immense and immovable, a group of shorebirds, snowy plovers, scurry along the edge of a sunlit mudflat, their tiny legs a blur. They pick at the wet earth, run off, pick a little more. Farther out, on open water, rafts of ducks are preening and gabbling, and the silhouettes of still more birds—stilt, ibis, avocet—are visible across this green expanse, a river delta of 74,000 acres. Every desert must have an oasis. Here, it is the Bear River and its namesake refuge, an essential place for birds and the people who love them.

HISTORY

The birds have always come here, often in numbers that astound. Nowadays, about 33,000 people come here each year, too. The European explorer John Fremont in 1843 described tremendous flocks of waterfowl generating "a noise like thunder." Three years later Brigham Young led his Mormon exiles over the mountains to found Salt Lake City.

Settlement brought intensive agriculture, and with it large-scale water diversion projects along the Bear River; by 1920, perhaps 3,000 of the river delta's original 45,000 acres of marshland remained. A massive die-off of waterfowl from avian botulism that same year raised conservation awareness. Eight years later,

Congress established the river delta as the Bear River Migratory Bird Refuge.

In 1982, the Great Salt Lake began to rise; a year later its highly saline waters topped refuge dikes, killing marsh vegetation and inundating refuge buildings and infrastructure. By June of 1986, the sea had enlarged itself from 1,640 square miles to some 2,450. The refuge was all but erased. A diversion project began the following year, in which Great Salt Lake water was pumped westward to an evaporation pond on the Bonneville Salt Flats. Refuge dikes reappeared in 1989, and a massive restoration effort commenced then, with employees and volunteers clearing debris, building new water-control structures, and restoring visitor amenities;

Canada goose nest, Bear River Migratory Bird Refuge

between 1993 and 1994, land acquisitions added 9,000 acres of upland and wetland habitats.

Today, although salts deposited by the flood are diminished and marsh plants and birds are again on the upswing, the resurrection of this refuge is not quite complete. Bear River's corps of ardent supporters, including an active Friends organization, have launched a fundraising effort for a beautiful new Visitor Education Center, to be located near I-15, with a host of interpretive exhibits and facilities to benefit visitors and area schoolchildren.

GETTING THERE

From Brigham City, on I-15, take the Forest St. exit and travel west about 15 mi. to the refuge.

■ **SEASON:** Open year-round.
■ **HOURS:** Sunrise to sunset.
■ **FEES:** None.
■ **ADDRESS:** Bear River Refuge, Brigham City, UT 84302
■ **TELEPHONE:** 435/723-5887

TOURING BEAR RIVER

■ **BY AUTOMOBILE:** A 12-mile self-guided auto tour is open daily, sunrise to sunset (closed January through mid-March).
■ **BY FOOT:** Walking is permitted along the 12-mile refuge auto-tour route (see "by automobile"). An observation deck is available; future plans include more decks and tour routes, some of which will accommodate visitors on foot.

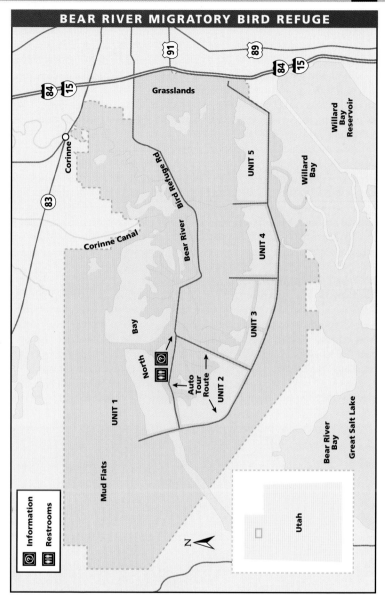

■ BY BICYCLE: Biking is allowed along the refuge auto-tour route only.
■ BY CANOE, KAYAK, OR BOAT: Boating is not permitted except during hunting seasons. Bear River Channel is open to public boating upstream from the old Refuge Headquarters site, year-round.

WHAT TO SEE

■ LANDSCAPE AND CLIMATE Bear River lies on the eastern edge of the Great Basin, a tremendously varied arid region encompassing 186,000 square miles of Utah, Nevada, and California. Utah's Wasatch Mountains form the basin's eastern rim, and the Sierra Nevada Range of California bounds it on the west; a great many interior ranges further divide the basin into smaller valleys and deserts, including Death Valley in southwest California, the basin's lowest point.

In Utah the basin's dominant feature is the Great Salt Lake. It is a remnant of two immense glacial lakes, Bonneville and Lahontan, born in the Pleistocene epoch. The lake today receives freshwater from the Bear, Weber, and Jordan rivers, although it has no outlet. Brine shrimp flourish in its waters, which are far more saline than the world's oceans. Bounding the lake are expanses of salt flats, hard as pavement, formed by evaporating lake water interacting with minerals and sedimentary rock.

At the refuge, the Bear River spills across the valley floor to meet the Great Salt Lake, forming an estuary environment. Undiluted saltwater is lethal to most wetland vegetation, although a number of plant species have adapted to tolerate higher levels. Prolific snowfall in surrounding mountains recharges the Bear and other rivers each spring; in the valley, however, an arid climate prevails. Spring and fall are mild, the summers moderately hot, with average high temperatures into the 90s; winters are dry and cold, at times extremely so, with average lows in the mid-20s.

■ PLANT COMMUNITIES

Wetlands The refuge offers several variations—both natural and human-induced—on a wetlands theme, some of which involve the commingling of freshwater and saltwater. Impoundments maintain open water at depths of a few inches to several feet depending on the seasonal requirements of bird species; one important goal is to provide optimal depth for the growth of sago pondweed, by far the most important waterfowl food here, as all parts of the plant are consumed. Small fish, eaten by herons and other birds, inhabit some refuge pools. Adjoining the shallows are labyrinths of emergent vegetation, including alkali and hardstem bul-

Sora rail

rush, glasswort, and, moving from wet into moist areas, grasses such as common reed and foxtail barley. Extensive mudflats harbor a wealth of invertebrates, including brine flies and midges, a dietary staple for many shorebirds.

■ **ANIMAL LIFE** Here it is birdlife. A few mammals are present, such as red fox, yellow-bellied marmot, and muskrat, but they are seldom seen. Birds, on the other hand, present an ebb and flow of beauty and surprises throughout the year. Wetlands continue to redevelop in the aftermath of the flood, with species numbers and diversity following suit.

The spring and fall displays of migrating shorebirds, herons, and waterfowl are magnificent. Tundra swans appear in October and November in numbers to 50,000 or more. Ducks—goldeneye, American wigeon, lesser scaup, bufflehead—appear in great numbers. The eared grebe and sandhill crane are common migrants; present but less readily seen are the canvasback duck and common loon. Migrant shorebirds include the solitary and Baird's sandpipers, marbled godwit, black-bellied plover, and long-billed dowitcher. At Bear River serious birders have a chance of spotting many rarities—whimbrel, dunlin, stilt sandpiper, American golden plover, and ruddy turnstone, among others.

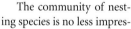
Whimbrel

The community of nesting species is no less impressive. Some of the showiest of shorebirds—willets, American avocet, black-necked stilt, long-billed curlew—are prolific here. Arriving in April and May, their young are darting along mudflats and shorelines by June or July. Also abundant are wading birds—the great blue heron, white-faced ibis, snowy and cattle egret, and black-crowned nightheron will be seen by most any visitor. Other marsh devotees—the sora and Virginia rail, black tern, Caspian tern—nest here but are less conspicuous. American white pelicans are common in summer as well, although they nest on an island in the Great Salt Lake. Eight species of duck nest on-site, the most common of which are ruddy duck, gadwall, and cinnamon teal. Nesting grebes include the Clark's, western, eared, and pied-billed.

Winter is a good time to see raptors. Bald eagles may arrive by the hundreds in January, loafing on the frozen flats and fishing for carp; the prairie falcon, rough-legged hawk, northern goshawk, ferruginous hawk, merlin, sharp-shinned and Cooper's hawk may all pay a visit, some species in great numbers. The peregrine falcon and golden eagle are here year-round but not in large numbers.

Other rarities are possible in the cold months. Ducks such as old-squaw, surf scoter, wood duck, and hooded merganser and shorebirds such as sanderling and several gulls—Thayer's, glaucous, and herring—may be seen.

Songbird migration, formerly a notable time, has diminished with the loss of willow thickets and nonnative trees to the flood. Red-winged and yellow-headed blackbirds and the western meadowlark remain fixtures in the marshes; in grassland areas, the sage thrasher and Brewer's sparrow nest here in summer but are more commonly seen here during migration.

ACTIVITIES

■ **CAMPING:** Camping is not permitted on the refuge, but there are private campgrounds in Brigham, Willard, and Mantua.

■ **SWIMMING:** Not permitted.

■ **WILDLIFE OBSERVA-TION:** Binoculars are essential here; a spotting scope is

Western grebe

very useful, given the great expanses of river delta and limited opportunities for foot travel. The parched, saline ground reflects light brightly; so bring along a hat and sunglasses.

■ **PHOTOGRAPHY:** Two permanent photo blinds are currently under construction. With proper equipment—meaning long or zoom lenses—this is a premier environment for photographing shorebirds. Sunsets are memorable.

■ **SEASONAL EVENTS:** May: Great Salt Lake Bird Festival, Great Bear River Refuge Festival; International Migratory Bird Day, National Wetlands Week.

■ **PUBLICATIONS:** General refuge brochure; refuge bird checklist; state of Utah bird checklist; children's bird list; plant list; *Migrations,* a quarterly publication of the Friends of Bear River Migratory Bird Refuge.

HUNTING AND FISHING
Waterfowl and **upland-game** hunting permitted during state seasons; special regulations apply. Fishing is permitted at the old headquarters site only.

Fish Springs NWR
Dugway, Utah

Wintering trumpeter swans walking on ice, Fish Springs NWR

To arrive at 17,992-acre Fish Springs NWR is to find the improbable beauty of a natural oasis—its jewel-like springs of turquoise and jade green are lively with fish and lush vegetation and noisy with birdlife.

HISTORY

Fish Springs has many ghosts. In the mid-1800s, it served as a way station for both the Overland Stage Route and Pony Express. Next came the Transcontinental Telegraph System, and in the early 1900s the Lincoln Highway, the first road linking New York and California. Historic photos, shattered segments of road, and listing, telegraph poles are all part of the experience here.

GETTING THERE

A minor challenge, met each year by about 2,700 visitors. Be sure to have a spare tire and a full tank of gas, and call ahead for road conditions. From the town of Delta, UT, travel north on UT 6 to County Rd. 174; turn left (west) and continue 40 mi. on a paved route until reaching a 'Y' in the road; bear right onto a dirt road (at refuge sign here) and continue approximately 15 mi. to a 'T' in the road; turn left and continue 5 mi. to refuge entrance.

■ **SEASON:** Open year-round.

■ **HOURS:** Daylight hours; refuge headquarters open weekdays, 8 a.m.–4:30 p.m.

■ **FEES:** None.

■ **ADDRESS:** P.O. Box 568, Dugway, UT 84022

■ **TELEPHONE:** 435/831-5353

TOURING FISH SPRINGS

■ **BY AUTOMOBILE:** Visitors may drive all refuge roads, incuding an 11-mile self-guided auto-tour route open year-round. Any closed roads will be marked with signs.

■ **BY FOOT:** Walking is permitted on most refuge lands and roads between July 16 and May 14. A portion of the refuge south of headquarters is closed to all access, and Gadwall and Ibis pools are closed as well. During the eight-week nesting closure, foot travel is restricted to the refuge auto tour.

■ **BY BICYCLE:** Biking is flat here and is permitted on all refuge roads open to vehicles except during the eight-week nesting closure, May 15– July 15. It's also hot, and drinking water is available outside refuge headquarters.

■ **BY CANOE, KAYAK, OR BOAT:** Permitted between July 16 and May 15 on all refuge ponds except Gadwall and Ibis and during nesting closure. Boating is a good means of exploring the numerous islands dotting larger ponds and marshlands.

WHAT TO SEE

■ **LANDSCAPE AND CLIMATE** Fish Springs lies at an elevation of 4,300 feet on the southern edge of the Great Salt Lake Desert, the vast lakebed of glacial Lake Bonneville. A desert climate prevails, with annual precipitation averaging only 8 inches and a lightning-quick evaporation rate. A series of warm, saline springs is the outstanding natural feature here. Water temperatures vary from 70 to 80 degrees year-round, with flows sufficient to maintain 10,000 acres of shallow salty water impoundments.

■ PLANT LIFE AND HABITATS

Wetlands Wet meadows of salt grass, alkali sacaton, and common reed occur here, along with spike rush and wire rush. Permanent marshes feature hardstem bulrush and Olney's bulrush. Among submergent plants are coontail, wigeongrass, and muskgrass. A seasonal drying cycle is maintained, which keeps wetlands productive. With constant moisture, needed decomposition does not occur properly. Drying returns oxygen and other nutrients to the soil, which promotes plant and insect growth, which attracts and increases the abundance of ducks.

Arid lands Desert shrublands at Fish Springs display several species of horse-

Marsh, Fish Springs NWR

brush and shad scale, as well as Mormon's tea and Anderson's lycium, the dominant woody varieties. Globe mallow, evening primrose, prickly pear cactus, and desert paintbrush are present in some areas; dominant grasses include Indian ricegrass and cheatgrass.

■ ANIMAL LIFE

Birds Nominated as a site of regional importance in the Western Hemispheric Shorebird Reserve Network, Fish Springs is a vital stopover for migrating shorebirds, waterfowl, and wading birds. Several lovely species from these groups nest on-site—black-necked stilt, canvasback, and snowy egret, among others—but the greatest diversity occurs in mid-April and late September. Golden eagles may be seen year-round.

Mammals Look for desert cottontail, bushy-tailed woodrat, antelope ground squirrel, and pronghorn.

Reptiles and amphibians A tremendous show of reptiles includes the Great Basin sagebrush lizard, collared and desert side-blotched lizard, Great Basin gopher snake, and the Great Basin rattlesnake. All are common.

Fish The Utah chub, a dietary staple for many birds, is prolific in spring. The mosquito fish and speckled dace, both introduced species, are present as well, as is the least chub, a species of special concern; reintroduction of this fish is under way.

ACTIVITIES

■ **CAMPING:** Camping is not permitted on the refuge; very primitive camping is available on Bureau of Land Mangement (BLM) lands, which surround the refuge.

■ **SWIMMING:** No swimming is allowed at Fish Springs.

■ **WILDLIFE OBSERVATION AND PHOTOGRAPHY:** In terms of visitor comfort and wildlife activity, fall and spring are the prime seasons at Fish Springs. With long lenses, this is an excellent site for images of nesting snowy egret, black-crowned night-heron, and white-faced ibis; Mallard Pool is a prime spot for bird-watching.

■ **HIKES AND WALKS:** Other than the auto-tour route, the refuge has no designated or marked walking trails. Drive north of refuge headquarters one mile and turn left at a Pony Express marker onto a dirt road, which winds up into a scenic canyon. Lands to the south of the road are part of a BLM Wilderness Study Area—tremendous hiking is here, along with abundant desert wildlife.

■ **SEASONAL EVENTS:** May: International Migratory Bird Day; September: Refuge open house (third Saturday), with free airboat rides, birding tours, talks on the Pony Express Trail, and other local history.

■ **PUBLICATIONS:** Refuge brochure, with map; refuge bird checklist; state of Utah bird checklist.

Ouray NWR
Vernal, Utah

Canada geese

Leota Bluff, like several other similar bluffs at Ouray NWR, is a wonderfully strange, multihued hump of sandstone and shale, well baked in summer, deep frozen in winter. In the soft light of morning or dusk, subtle bands of cinnamon, ivory, ochre, and yellow-browns streak the sandstone, the handiwork of ancient seas and rising mountains, weather and time.

Supreme hunters perch upon these bluffs. Golden eagles, like people, desire a view, though for purposes more essential than a snapshot. It's hard even to imagine how an eagle might regard the expanse below—the broad, verdant floodplain of the Green River with its stately groves of cottonwood, the river colored slate gray, cutting a large horseshoe bend across the refuge, with a mirror image of weathered bluffs in the distance—but given their presence at Ouray throughout the year, there can be no doubt that they see their home.

As do so many other creatures who inhabit this largely untrammeled landscape set in a climate of extremes. Temperatures in the high desert are always on the move in one direction or another, it seems, and moving quickly, like the shadow of an eagle on the wing.

HISTORY

The Uinta Basin and surrounding lands were the presettlement home of the Ute Indians, who live today on the Uintah and Ouray reservation, adjoining the refuge to the south. About 2,700 acres of refuge lands are leased from the tribe. Visitors should be aware of reservation boundaries and remember that off-road travel on tribal lands is not allowed without first obtaining a permit. (For hunting, camping, and recreational activities, contact the Tribal Offices in Fort Duchesne at 435/722-0877.)

Ouray was established in 1960 with the goal of providing habitat for migratory birds, primarily ducks and geese. But things are slowly changing. This region of

Utah, a part of the Upper Colorado Ecosystem, has never functioned naturally as a major waterfowl breeding ground. Its more vital role is that of a migratory corridor for birds of all kinds, from sandhill cranes to songbirds. The Green River's abundant floodplain forests and river-maintained wetlands are the important pieces of this natural system. Today refuge management has as its primary goal the long-term maintenance of these habitats for resting and feeding migrants, as well as conserving the natural diversity of native species in its intact desert shrubland community.

An ongoing problem here has been contamination of some refuge ponds and marshes by selenium, which may have leached into the watershed. There are natural selenium deposits in the area, and run-off water from nearby farm fields simply carries more of the mineral to the refuge. Toxic (in sufficient quantities) to most any living thing, selenium first appeared in the 1980s in ponds near the refuge entrance. The refuge is moving animals to areas with a lesser concentration of selenium and is controlling the situation by planting trees and allowing cattails to grow wild in areas where the selenium has been recorded in higher concentrations.

GETTING THERE

From Vernal, UT, travel west on US 40 for 15 mi., turning left (south) onto UT 88; continue 13 mi. to refuge entrance.
- **SEASON:** Open year-round.
- **HOURS:** Open daylight hours. Refuge headquarters, with literature and some exhibits, open weekdays, 7:30 a.m.–4 p.m.
- **FEES:** None.
- **ADDRESS:** 266 W. 100 N. #2, Vernal, UT 84078
- **TELEPHONE:** 435/789-0351

TOURING OURAY

- **BY AUTOMOBILE:** Driving is permitted on refuge auto-tour route and unimproved roads year-round. The 12-mile self-guided auto-tour route offers good migratory-bird and deer and elk sightings; the Leota Bluffs overlook provides a beautiful view of the entire refuge. Roads turn to gumbo following a rain, although they dry quickly, usually within a day. Accessing some of the less-traveled roads here requires a high-clearance or 4WD vehicle.
- **BY FOOT:** Walking is allowed year-round on refuge roads and lands; some closed areas are marked with signs. While there are no designated

Black-necked stilt

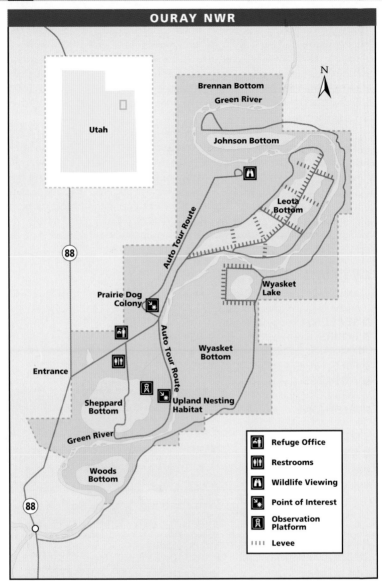

OURAY NWR

Brennan Bottom

Green River

Johnson Bottom

Utah

Leota
Bottom

Auto Tour Route

88

Wyasket
Lake

Prairie Dog
Colony

Auto Tour Route

Wyasket
Bottom

Entrance

Sheppard
Bottom

Upland Nesting
Habitat

Green River

Woods
Bottom

88

🏢	**Refuge Office**
🚻	**Restrooms**
👁	**Wildlife Viewing**
✳	**Point of Interest**
🪧	**Observation Platform**
׀׀׀׀	**Levee**

or improved trails, Ouray offers superb opportunities for solitude and exploration. About 7,500 visitors come to Ouray each year.

■ **BY BICYCLE:** Biking is permitted on refuge auto-tour route and levee roads year-round. It may not be the best way to see wildlife, but during the cooler times of the day, it offers a good workout in a beautiful landscape. Roads are extremely muddy and slick following a rain.

■ **BY CANOE, KAYAK, OR BOAT:** A raft float or canoe trip on the Green River promises a memorable encounter with the region's geologic wonders, wildlife, and quiet spaces. Many floaters put in at Dinosaur National Monument, upriver, entering the refuge at trip's end. A takeout at Ouray Bridge is located on the Uintah and Ouray Indian Reservation; a tribal permit is required in advance for use of the takeout, or for floaters who wish to continue downriver through reservation land. Strong headwinds on the river are common; pack lots of water and mosquito repellent.

■ **BY HORSEBACK:** Horseback riding is permitted on the refuge auto-tour route and levee roads year-round.

WHAT TO SEE

■ **LANDSCAPE AND CLIMATE** Ouray lies within the Uinta Basin, which is little more than a dimple on the 50,000-square-mile Colorado Plateau, an upthrust table encompassing portions of Utah, New Mexico, Colorado, and Arizona. East of the plateau are the southern Rocky Mountains; the Great Basin sprawls to the west. On the northern skyline are the massive Uinta Mountains. Encompassing more than 100 miles, the Uintas are one of the few North American ranges trending east to west.

The Green River is the lifeblood of Ouray. South of here it all but vanishes from the horizon line, slicing through a series of spectacular canyons cut through the soft sedimentary rock of the Colorado Plateau. On the refuge, however, the Green's trench is shallow and broad. Natural flooding is still a possibility here each spring, due in part to the undammed Yampa River, which meets the Green just upstream from the refuge. Harnessed by Flaming Gorge Dam in Wyoming, most every aspect of the Green's ecology has been altered.

Uinta Basin soils include loose conglomerations of sand and viscous oil, along with natural gas. In the Wonsit Valley to the east, oil and gas derricks plumb these deposits, most of which are quite shallow.

Ouray's arid climate features just 7.4 inches of precipitation annually, most of it falling as rain, with June and July typically the wettest months. Snowfall is minimal and usually occurs between December and March. Daytime highs may exceed 50 degrees through the winter months, but nighttime readings can be bru-

Black bear: boar, sow, and cub

tal, with lows of minus-30; overall, it's cold enough that the Green River often freezes solid. Summers are hot, with daytime highs of 100 or more common, followed by cool to cold nights.

■ PLANT LIFE AND HABITATS

Wetlands The term "moist-soil unit" has a bureaucratic ring. It's a controlled wetland, a concept gaining favor on refuges with rivers, especially where the flooding cycle has been extinguished by dams. In 1997 Ouray put 50 acres into moist-soil units. Swamped in spring, the area is then slowly drained. Alkali bulrush rises up, and shorebird and waterfowl delicacies—fairy and clam shrimp, and many insects—proliferate in the warm water. Encouraged by the results thus far, the refuge is experimenting with different flooding-and-drying cycles to learn how aquatic plants and invertebrates respond.

The largest share of wetlands is the historic floodplain of the Green River, with dikes creating separate marshes. The mix varies from deeper, open water to impenetrable thickets of cattail and hardstem bulrush, to wet fringes of spike rushes and wire grass; unwanted exotic plants such as tamarisk are also present. Smartweed and several varieties of dock are major submergent plants. Prior to damming, high water delivered the larvae and fry of fish (small, especially young, recently hatched fish) into these shallow pools, which provided a nursery where they developed before later escaping into the river. This process is important for the endangered razorback sucker. Ouray is attempting to mimic that natural cycle by breaching some levees, restoring flows into and out of marshes in an effort to aid the fish.

Woodlands About 1,282 acres of Ouray consist of woodlands bounding the refuge's 12-mile stretch of the Green River. Important trees include Fremont's cottonwood, peach-leaf willow, and whiplash willow, with an understory of silver buffalo berry, squawbush, and many exotic species—tamarisk, pepperweed, giant whitetop, and Russian olive, among others. Whitetop and tamarisk, also known as

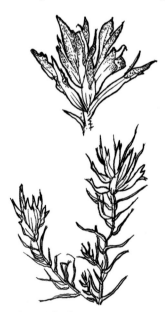

Indian paintbrush

salt cedar, are ecologic terrors. They enjoy salt-rich soils and the long growing season, offer minimal value to wildlife, and ruthlessly outcompete native plants. Once established, they're extremely difficult to remove. Refuge workers hack the stuff down, spray it with herbicides, burn it, with marginal success. Ouray's management staff says more intensive control efforts are urgently needed.

Arid lands Ouray's 2,189 acres of semi-arid shrublands abound with the unyielding beauty of big sagebrush, black sagebrush, rubber and low rabbit brush, greasewood, spiny hopsage, and four-wing saltbush. Indian ricegrass, sand dropseed, and needle-and-thread are major grasses. The threatened Uinta Basin hookless cactus survives here; a 1997 survey revealed some 2,100 cacti present. Not much is known about the life history or specific requirements of this plant, which at Ouray favors the graveled terraces of upland sites.

Other habitats About 1,000 acres of grasslands, with such species as western wheatgrass, inland salt grass, and Great Basin wild rye, occupy the refuge. Wildflowers here include scarlet globe mallow, desert paintbrush, and several goldenrod varities.

Wildlife utilize everything, even Ouray's 1,461 acres of barren clay bluffs. The caves and crevices here provide winter den sites for a thriving community of snakes and lizards, and handy perches for hawks, eagles, and falcons. Bats may also use caves, although this has yet to be confirmed.

Just 157 acres of Ouray feature croplands, with alfalfa, barley, and sorghum planted on a rotation basis; the crops feed many birds, rodents, and hoofed mammals, which in turn feed predators.

■ ANIMAL LIFE

Birds A number of rare or uncommon species make Ouray their home. Sightings of peregrine falcons have increased, and a visitor in spring or fall stands a fair chance of spotting one. Four species of management concern—the Swainson's hawk, long-billed curlew, and Lewis' woodpecker—nest on-site. Other rare birds occurring here include the ferruginous hawk, yellow-billed cuckoo, northern goshawk, Caspian tern, blue grosbeak, and southwestern willow flycatcher. Sage grouse, extremely rare, are found in shrubland areas. Bald eagles arrive in fall and remain through January or early February.

Many beautiful birds are common at Ouray. The white-faced ibis, black-necked stilt, and lesser yellowlegs, and Wilson's phalarope ply the shallow marsh edges. Widespread are the orange-crowned and Virgina warblers, white-throated swift, Say's phoebe, and rock wren. Golden eagles are present throughout the year, and many waterfowl species—green-winged teal, American wigeon, redhead, northern shoveler, and ruddy duck—are reliably present spring through fall.

Goshawk in nest

Yellow-bellied marmot

Uncommon nesting species here include the rufous-sided towhee, warbling vireo, yellow-breasted chat, and loggerhead shrike. The sage sparrow, sage thrasher, green-tailed towhee, ash-throated flycatcher, lazuli bunting, and black-headed grosbeak are present in very limited numbers and not easily seen.

Mammals White behinds, big racks: The mule deer and its 800-pound cousin, the elk, frequent Ouray fall through spring and are readily observed. Elk first appeared in the winter of 1997; refuge staff believe they migrate in from the Roan Cliffs and East Tavaputs Plateau to the south. The northern river otter, a species of management concern, is an increasing presence in the Green River and adjoining marshlands. Otters are great fishermen, and the refuge is home to endangered river species such as the razorback sucker, the Colorado pike minnow, the hump-back chub, and bonytail chub. Mountain lions den in the barren clay hills, and two bat species—the Mexican free-tailed and Townsend's big-eared—are also suspected of using this area. Moose and black bear visit the river on occasion; beaver, muskrat, white-tailed and black-tailed jackrabbits, along with coyote, raccoon, and Ord's kangaroo rat, are all quite common. Always engaging are the squirrels—the white-tailed antelope squirrel, white-tailed prairie dog, yellow-bellied marmot, and least chipmunk. All inhabit the drier, open shrublands and grasslands.

Reptiles and amphibians In shrubland areas and rocky slopes you may spot three species of lizards—the eastern fence, side-blotched, and short-horned. Other snakes are more readily seen, such as the Great Basin gopher snake and wandering garter snake; the western whiptail and western rattlesnake are present as well.

Fish Several imperiled fish species survive in this stretch of the Green River: humpback chub, bonytail chub, Colorado pike minnow, and razorback sucker. Most are in severe decline. Alteration of water temperature and river flows by the Flaming Gorge Dam is the principal culprit. In 1996 Ouray National Fish Hatchery began propagating young of these species for release into the Green and other rivers. A great variety of nonnative fish are also present: smallmouth bass, sand shiner, channel catfish, yellow perch, northern pike, rainbow and brown trout, and green sunfish.

ACTIVITIES

■ **CAMPING:** Camping is not permitted on the refuge, but numerous opportunities are available in the town of Dinosaur, near Dinosaur National Monument, about 50 miles east (435/789-2115).

■ **WILDLIFE OBSERVATION AND PHOTOGRAPHY:** On the whole, spring (March-May) and fall (September-November) are the most productive and enjoyable times to visit. Wildflower displays in the shrublands and grasslands are beautiful and usually peak in June. Songbirds, pelicans, and other wildlife frequent the sandbars and thickets here.

HUNTING AND FISHING Ouray offers hunting for **mule deer**, **pheasants**, **ducks**, and **geese**. Deer hunting occurs during Utah's scheduled archery, extended archery, rifle, and muzzle-loader seasons. Waterfowl hunting generally occurs between Oct. and Jan.—it's not uncommon, however, for refuge marshes to be frozen by early to mid-Dec. Pheasant hunting generally happens in Nov.

Fishing is permitted on the Green River. **Channel catfish** are among the most sought-after species here; other fish in the Green include **black crappie**, **bluegill**, **smallmouth bass**, **black bullhead**, among many others. Endangered fish—razorback sucker, bonytail and humpback chub, Colorado pikeminnow—must be returned unharmed to the river.

There are tremendous opportunities for scenic images—Ouray's domed bluffs of shale and sandstone reveal many colorful layers in early-morning or late-evening light. The refuge is also a good site for larger animals such as deer and elk; mule deer bucks in this area are renowned for their large, regal antlers, and does with fawns are often spotted in early summer.

PUBLICATIONS: Refuge brochure with map; auto-tour brochure; refuge bird checklist; state of Utah bird checklist.

National Elk Refuge
Jackson Hole, Wyoming

American elk herd, National Elk Refuge

At dawn the snow in the valley is pale violet; on the deeply chiseled walls of the Tetons, there is the hint of daylight, glowing embers of soft reds and golds. A few stars remain overhead. It's a cold, windless morning, with temperatures hovering around 16 below zero. Across the expanse of winter meadow only a few clumps of grass poke through. The elk are lying quietly, long legs tucked beneath their massive bodies to conserve heat. Their silhouettes appear in groups ranging from three or four to 50, adult cows, small yearlings, mature bulls with huge, backswept antlers, gnarled like tree limbs.

There may be 7,000 elk here this morning on the National Elk Refuge, the largest concentrated wintering herd in the world. They roam the wild country to the north, where they thrive in spring, summer, and fall. During winter, which can last a hard five to six months, they crowd onto this 25,000-acre refuge and adjoining lands in the valley. Hemmed in by mountains on one side and the town of Jackson on the other, there is no room to move. But most of them survive.

HISTORY

A dramatic and compact high-mountain valley, Jackson Hole provided winter range for as many as 25,000 elk when settlement began in the 1890s. By the turn of the century, the herd's historic range was being converted to hay fields, crops, and a small townsite. Great numbers of elk had always perished in severe winters—an 1897 account claims "not less" than 10,000 died that year—but the winters of 1909-11 brought the future of human-wildlife coexistence into sharp focus. Famished elk broke down fences and devoured hay set aside for livestock. Winter mortalities were high. Landowners, while not without concern for the animals, faced serious economic hardship, and made their frustrations known.

The idea for a permanent elk refuge came in 1906 from D.C. Nowlin, state game warden of Wyoming. By 1910, elk-landowner conflicts were severe enough to force the state legislature to purchase all available hay in the valley to feed the herd. The following year, Wyoming received $20,000 from Congress for supplemental feeding, along with a promise to investigate. The National Elk Refuge, comprising about 2,700 acres, was established in 1912, with Nowlin as manager.

The early refuge functioned as a feedlot. Hay was made available, and elk gathered to eat it. In years before this artificial feeding began, elk packed into the valley only during the coldest, snowiest months. Nowlin observed, in 1922, "eleven years of continuous feeding have virtually domesticated the elk ... [they] now come for hay regularly and early in the season, and we have been unable to accumulate a supply of hay sufficient for hard winters." If a remnant herd was to survive, Nowlin concluded, more refuge land was essential.

Eager for the government to solve the problem of elk damage to crops and fences, ranchers were bitterly opposed to federal land acquisition. Some accused the refuge of deliberately mismanaging the herd in order to bankrupt them. Efforts to establish and later expand Grand Teton National Park beyond the main Teton Range met with similar opposition. What nobody hollered about was this: The Jackson elk herd, a public asset, yielded substantial private profit. Dude ranches and guided hunting trips meant good money for landowners and other residents. Expanding the refuge and national park might curtail, or more closely regulate, these activities. Today Grand Teton is the only national park where hunting is permitted, a trade-off rooted in the conflicts of the 1920s.

Through the following decades, the size of the Jackson elk herd became the focal point for debate. A 1974 agreement between the refuge and the Wyoming Game & Fish Dept. (WGFD), still in effect today, calls for a maximum winter herd of 7,500 animals on the refuge. The figure was derived from an 80-year average, "consistent with historical, political, economic, social, and biological realities," according to refuge literature.

The state wildlife agency, dependent upon hunter license sales and lobbied by a powerful outfitter-and-guide industry, presides over an annual regional harvest of 3,000 or so elk. Economic benefits of the hunt ripple through Jackson. Add

Gray wolves

photographers and other tourists who arrive in search of elk, and the annual value of the herd tops $12 million.

If the National Elk Refuge had begun with its present acreage of 25,000, along with adjacent national forest lands, supplemental winter feeding might never have been necessary. Management of refuge grasslands has increased annual forage to 21,000 tons, enough to sustain 5,000 elk through the winter. Refuge officials would like to see a herd of this size; but supplemental feeding, too, is institutionalized, with WGFD a leading proponent. The herd forages naturally between October and late January, and receives pellets of alfalfa through early April. Supplemental feeding costs $300,000-450,000, annually. There is no question feeding modifies elk behavior, at least through the winter. The herd is far more tolerant of people than wintering wild elk in other areas.

Between 1985 and 1997, the limited objective of 7,500 wintering elk on the refuge went out the window. Herd numbers escalated; as many as 10,000 animals appeared on the refuge, with 9,000 more on other land in the valley. Shoulder to shoulder at the refuge feed line, occasionally mingling with horses and livestock around Jackson, concerns rose about the spread of diseases—pasteurellosis, brucellosis, tuberculosis. TB poses an especially serious threat. Symptoms may not appear for months or several years though infected animals are contagious. Outbreaks of TB developed in herds of captive elk on game farms in the region in the early 1990s. Famous for their ability to thwart fences, one runaway elk could trigger an outbreak in the wild.

Does the system work? How many elk ought to be wintering on the refuge and in the valley as a whole? Summer range in Grand Teton National Park and adjoining national forest lands is capable of sustaining 10-20,000 elk. They are an important food source for predators such as wolves, mountain lions, grizzly bears, and for carrion eaters such as wolverines. The problem remains *winter* habitat.

Some biologists and wildlife advocates have called for an end to supplemental

Bull elk with mature antlers

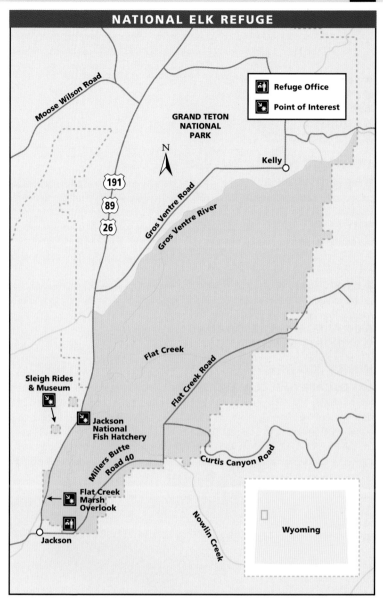

NATIONAL ELK REFUGE

- Refuge Office
- Point of Interest

Moose Wilson Road

GRAND TETON NATIONAL PARK

N

Kelly

191

89

26

Gros Ventre Road

Gros Ventre River

Flat Creek

Flat Creek Road

Sleigh Rides & Museum

Jackson National Fish Hatchery

Millers Butte Road 40

Curtis Canyon Road

Flat Creek Marsh Overlook

Jackson

Nowlin Creek

Wyoming

feeding on the refuge. A "cold turkey" approach would lower the herd to an estimated 4-6,000, but the spectacle of mass starvation, which caused early residents so much distress, is not appealing. In 1999 the WGFD was suing the National Elk Refuge, contending that in order to fulfill its mission of wildlife management, it must be allowed to come onto refuge grounds and carry out whatever program it deems necessary—vaccinating elk against diseases, and, presumeably, conducting supplemental feeding, should the refuge decide to some day curtail it.

Big animals with big antlers in big herds. Big winters in big country. Big money and big disagreements. Borne of these uniquely western elements, the National Elk Refuge and its marquee seasonal residents will find a way to carry on.

GETTING THERE

Refuge headquarters, at 675 E. Broadway St., is 1 mi. east from Jackson's town square. Jackson Hole–Greater Yellowstone Visitor Center, with outstanding exhibits and a bookstore is on North Cache St., about 2 mi. north of town square, off US 191.

- **SEASON:** Open year-round.
- **HOURS:** Open daylight hours.
- **FEES:** None.
- **ADDRESS:** P.O. Box 510, Jackson, WY 83001
- **TELEPHONE:** 307/733-9212

TOURING NATIONAL ELK REFUGE

- **BY AUTOMOBILE:** Driving is permitted year-round on 4 miles of the main refuge road and adjoining highways. The main refuge road beyond the four-mile mark is closed from December 1 through April 30.
- **BY FOOT:** Hiking is limited to refuge roads year-round. One designated trail beginning on refuge lands winds east into the Bridger-Teton National Forest and is open spring through fall. Unparalleled hiking and walking are available in Grand Teton National Park, next door.
- **BY BICYCLE:** Biking is permitted and very popular on improved roads and gravel refuge roads seasonally; mountain bike tours of the refuge are available at cycling tour companies in Jackson.
- **BY CANOE, KAYAK, OR BOAT:** Not permitted.
- **BY HORSE-DRAWN SLEIGH:** See "Seasonal Events."

WHAT TO SEE

LANDSCAPE AND CLIMATE The National Elk Refuge adjoins 310,000-acre Grand Teton National Park to the north; Grand Teton, in turn, borders 2.2-million-acre Yellowstone National Park. The eastern boundary of the refuge adjoins 3.4 million-acre Bridger-Teton National Forest. These public lands make up the core of the Greater Yellowstone Ecosystem, the most biologically intact region remaining in the lower 48 states. The vast majority of elk wintering on the refuge wander these lands during the balance of the year.

Wintering trumpeter swans, National Elk Refuge

A more inspiring scene is hard to find. From the flat Jackson Valley at 6,750 feet, steep-sided, enormous foothills rise into coniferous forest, and, finally, the granite crags of the Teton Range; eight peaks exceed 12,000 feet, with the tallest, Grand Teton, soaring to 13,700 feet. Geologically young, the Tetons reach beyond the tree line into alpine tundra, then barren rock. The valley and mountains display classic examples of glaciation; soils across the southern half of the refuge are rich in glacial outwash, with one prominent, erosion-resistant landmark, Miller Butte, standing 500 feet above the valley. Two streams, the Gros Ventre River and Flat Creek, traverse refuge lands, providing a good deal of open-water habitat and sustaining a fishery comprising of both native and introduced species.

The climate is typical of high-elevation valleys in the northern Rockies—cool, brief summers and lengthy winters. Annual snowfall on the refuge forms a gradient, with 6 to 8 inches accumulating across the southern half, and as much as 4 feet in the north; snow accounts for half the refuge's annual 15 inches of precipitation. Summer temperatures are generally pleasant, in the 80s to low 90s; winter extremes may reach 40 below zero, though milder temperatures in the 20s are fairly typical.

■ PLANT LIFE AND HABITATS

Grasslands More than 8,000 acres here are grasslands, the majority of which are nonnative tame species; some, such as Russian wild rye and intermediate wheatgrass, are stouter than native grasses and remain upright longer in snow, a characteristic benefitting the elk. Other exotics—brome, timothy, Kentucky bluegrass—were introduced by ranchers in pre-refuge days. Great Basin wild rye, a very tall, showy native, is seen along roadsides and scattered elsewhere. Through intensive management, including irrigation and prescribed burning, refuge grasslands produce enough standing forage each year to feed 5,000 elk during their six-month stay; deep, hard-crusted snow, however, puts much of this feed out of reach during the last four to six weeks of winter.

Arid lands South-facing slopes, rocky outcrops, and other sites on higher elevations feature a matrix of mountain shrub species interspersed with extensive sagebrush grasslands. There is an understory of needle-and-thread, bluebunch wheatgrass, and Indian ricegrass. Big sagebrush, bitterbrush, and rabbit brush are typical shrub species; wildflowers in the mix include arrowleaf balsamroot, Indian paintbrush, lupine, and pasqueflower, among others.

Forests Located primarily on the northern slopes and

Arrowleaf balsamroot

drainages of the Gros Ventre Hills, forested areas encompass some 2,400 acres; conifer species include Douglas fir and lodgepole pine, along with aspen parklands. Healthy aspen communities feature trees of diverse ages and understories of shrubs and grasses; as many as 10 species of mammals and 40 bird species depend on this habitat in Wyoming, second only to wetlands in terms of importance for wildlife. Here and elsewhere in Jackson Hole, aspen groves are declining. Suppression of wildfire, which stimulates aspen reproduction, along with occasionally heavy browsing by elk during winter and early spring, are contributing factors.

Along the Gros Ventre River is a lovely floodplain forest, including nonnative blue spruce, with narrowleaf cottonwood, red osier dogwood, and several varieties of willow. Elk have taken a substantial toll on the willow corridor along Flat Creek, and have affected cottonwood trees as well.

Wetlands Occupying scattered depressions in the valley floor and flanking the Gros Ventre River and lower reaches of Flat Creek are about 1,200 acres of ponds, marshes, and wet meadows. Cattail, sedges, and rushes are the dominant plant varieties. These areas, too, are utilized by hungry elk, and it's interesting to see the difference between grazed and ungrazed wetlands. Near the Visitor Center is an area of marsh fenced off from elk—compare the density of emergent vegetation here with most any other wetland site, where the animals are free to forage.

■ ANIMAL LIFE

Birds Known for its megafauna, the elk refuge also boasts a lively and diverse avian community. Swans are a presence year-round, with a nesting population of trumpeters and a wintering population of trumpeters and tundra swans. Bald and golden eagles are readily seen in the winter, scavenging elk carcasses. Nesting raptors on the refuge include the American kestrel, prairie falcon, and red-tailed hawk; golden eagles nest in nearby canyons. Sandhill cranes are quite common, along with such waterfowl as the Barrow's goldeneye. Wetlands and ponds feature yellow-headed blackbirds and marsh wrens.

Sagebrush shrublands and open grasslands are home to the sage grouse, Lincoln's sparrow, long-billed curlew, mountain bluebird, and sage thrasher. In forested areas, look for the Steller's and gray jays, ruffed grouse, tree swallow, ruby-crowned kinglet, MacGillivray's warbler, pine siskin, and mountain chickadee, among others.

Mammals The elk remain as long as possible in the highest mountain forests and meadows, moving downslope only as snow depths exceed several feet. Blasts of subzero air can provide the final incentive. A mature cow typically is the leader; each herd strings out single file, anywhere from 20 to 200 animals, and

Steller's jay

Horse-drawn sleigh ride for elk viewing

walks. They follow routes used by their ancestors over hundreds of years. The herds farthest away travel from the southern reaches of Yellowstone National Park, a one-way journey of up to 100 miles. The vast majority of cows have bred and are in the early stages of gestation.

By December the valley is in the grip of winter, and along the refuge road and highway north of Jackson, elk by the hundreds and even thousands are seen feeding, sparring, or resting quietly, chewing their cuds. The refuge is a winter haven for other species as well. The Jackson bison herd, 500 or more, is here through the coldest months. Moose, mule deer, and bighorn sheep are usually visible, the latter most frequently along the refuge's eastern boundary.

The herds attract predators and scavengers—coyotes, ravens, bald eagles, and the occasional mountain lion. In the winter of 1998-99, new players appeared. Producing pups and roaming ever more widely since being reintroduced to Yellowstone National Park, 11 gray wolves explored the valley and refuge. Those visiting here prospered. They ran down and killed 60 or so elk, a number of which were elderly, then moved on to the next order of wolf business, killing coyotes. In predawn light within 100 yards of the highway, wolves could be seen feeding on elk carcasses. A few visitors taking the sleigh ride witnessed wolves taking down elk. From late November through the end of March, the wolf may be observed conducting his business. Refuge management has no plans to intervene at this time; how many wolves come, and how many elk go, remains to be seen.

In summer the roster of mammals shrinks considerably. A few elk may be seen in predaylight hours on the north end of the refuge; pronghorn, moose, and mule deer are occasionally present. The coyote remains common, and many smaller species—beaver, badger, red squirrel, porcupine, long-tailed weasel, yellow pine chipmunk, Uinta ground squirrel, and western jumping mouse—occupy the refuge, most of them readily observable. River otter, however, are rare on refuge streams. The northern flying squirrel, though common in aspen and pine forests, is difficult to encounter here.

Fish Refuge streams support a wild population of native Snake River cutthroat trout; small numbers of introduced brook and rainbow trout are also present.

ACTIVITIES

■ **CAMPING:** Camping is not permitted on the refuge, but there are abundant opportunities on nearby national forest lands and in Grand Teton National Park.

■ **SWIMMING:** Swimming is permitted.

■ **WILDLIFE OBSERVATION:** The National Elk Refuge is a perfect place to become acquainted with several daunting, contentious wildlife management issues facing this splendidly wild region. Presently the refuge is a defendant in two lawsuits, one involving its refusal to allow WGFD management activities on refuge land; the other is an effort by the animal rights group Fund for Animals to prevent a limited bison hunt, which the refuge believes would assist in maintaining an optimal herd size. Wolves and controversy are seldom far apart; management of national forests and parks bordering the refuge comprises still another set of concerns. There are plenty more. Get informed and write a few letters.

> **HUNTING AND FISHING** Archery and firearm hunting of **elk** is permitted, generally from Oct. 16 through Dec. 5. Permits are obtained by attending a weekly public drawing; individuals must be present at drawing to qualify for a permit and must possess a Wyoming elk hunting license and valid hunter safety card.
>
> Fishing for **cutthroat trout**, **brook trout**, and **rainbow trout** is permitted on Gros Ventre River and designated sections of Upper Flat Creek, Lower Flat Creek, Nowlin Creek, and North "Elk" Park Pond.

■ **PHOTOGRAPHY:** Photographers of all skill levels who visit in winter will leave with terrific images of elk against the backdrop of a dramatic, primeval landscape. Refuge sleigh rides provide the casual photographer with an especially good opportunity for great shots.

■ **HIKES AND WALKS:** A beautiful walk may be had in late spring through late summer on a trail beginning at the northern edge of the refuge and winding uphill into the Teton National Forest.

■ **SEASONAL EVENTS:** December–March: A horse-drawn sleigh ride through the refuge is a popular tradition, offering close-up views of the elk herd and other wildlife on the refuge. Rides last about an hour, between 10 a.m. and 4 p.m., daily, departing from National Museum of Wildlife Art, 3 mles north of Jackson on US 191; no reservations; information: 307/733-9212.

January: Supplemental feeding of the herd usually commences in January, continues through late March, making elk easier to see.

May: Boy Scout Antler Auction. Local Boy Scouts collect shed antlers and hold an auction each spring in Jackson Hole; 80 percent of the funds raised are returned to the refuge for elk management and supplemental feeding.

■ **PUBLICATIONS:** Checklists of mammals and birds of Jackson Hole; brochures on refuge history, sleigh rides, elk biology and migration; refuge and elk fact sheet; *Wildlife Legacy: The National Elk Refuge,* outstanding color photographs and interpretive text.

Seedskadee NWR
Green River, Wyoming

Green River Lake, Wyoming

The music of Seedskadee is the song of a gentle landscape: the purr of the big riverside cottonwood trees combed by the wind; the bubbling of the glittering river underneath as it pours over riffles and gravel bars. On an August afternoon, everywhere else is hot. Within the tree-sheltered river corridor of 26,382-acre Seedskadee NWR, the moose and beavers and herons carry out their business in cool comfort, accompanied by the steady rhythms of the landscape.

HISTORY

Shoshone Indians called the Green River *Seedskadee,* meaning "river of the prairie hen," a reference to its abundant sage grouse. Pioneers on the Oregon, Mormon, and California trails passed over today's refuge, crossing the river at two ferry sites. Badly weathered remains of homesteader cabins and ranch buildings lie in remote areas of the refuge. A superb brochure interprets this rich history.

Seedskadee refuge was established in 1965 to mitigate for riverine and wetland habitats lost to the Fontenelle Dam. Equipped with a major irrigation system and downstream pumping station, the dam was designed to spur irrigated agricultural development, a vision never realized, due in part to poor soils. Today the dam serves primarily as a water-storage facility.

This refuge complex is growing; initial land purchases for a new refuge unit, Cokeville Meadows NWR, have begun, with a long-term goal of 25,000 acres of riverine habitats along the Bear River, two hours west of Seedskadee. And Seedskadee is popular, by Wyoming standards, with 17,000 visitors coming out each year.

GETTING THERE

From Rock Springs, WY, on I-80, travel west to the La Barge Rd. (US 372) exit. Continue north about 28 mi. on US 372, turning left at sign for refuge.

■ **SEASON:** Open year-round.

■ **HOURS:** Daylight hours; refuge headquarters open weekdays, 7:30 a.m.–4:30 p.m.; printed materials and restrooms in lobby accessible at all times.

■ **FEES:** None; special-use permits required for all commercial operations, such as river guiding and commercial photography.

■ **ADDRESS:** P.O. Box 700, Green River, WY 82935

■ **TELEPHONE:** 307/875-2187

TOURING SEEDSKADEE

■ **BY AUTOMOBILE:** Driving is permitted on refuge roads only, incuding an 8-mile self-guided auto tour that is open year-round. The roads provide good access and viewing of all major habitats; some roads, however, may be too rough for sedans.

■ **BY FOOT:** Walking is permitted year-round on designated refuge roads as indicated on current refuge brochure map, and most lands unless posted otherwise. The refuge has no designated trails at this time; two new developed trails are being planned.

■ **BY BICYCLE:** Biking is permitted on designated refuge roads only as indicated on current refuge brochure map.

■ **BY CANOE, KAYAK, OR BOAT:** Seeing the refuge by water is a terrific experience here; canoes, dories, and inflatable rafts are best. There are five launch areas on-site, with more upstream, outside the refuge. Trips from 3 to 14 hours are possible; it's a fast (but not hazardous) ride in spring, a sleepy float in late summer, with great wildlife viewing.

WHAT TO SEE

■ **LANDSCAPE AND CLIMATE** This is a high desert landscape, with climate, topography, and plant life more indicative of central Utah. Due north of Seedskadee some 170 miles are the Wind River Mountains, where the Green River rises. To the west are unique, aberrant landscapes: an expanse of 150-foot-high sand dunes and, just beyond the Great Divide Basin, a desolate, sun-scorched bowl encircled by low mountains, the result of a split in the Continental Divide.

Elevations vary just 300 feet across the refuge; the climate is semiarid, with just 7 inches of precipitation annually. Wind is a daily factor, beginning in the afternoons. Breezes are 10 to 12 mph and winds above 30 mph are not unusual; a light snowfall, accompanied by wind, will pack roads with drifts. Summers are fairly mild, with daytime highs in the upper 80s to low 90s, and cool nights.

Flowing 35 miles through the refuge, the Green River in this stretch is fairly swift and shallow, studded with boulders and bounded by occasional cliffs and eroded bluffs; a tributary, the Big Sandy River, enters the Green on the refuge. While spring flooding still occurs here, the Fontenelle Dam has caused the riverbed to deepen, creating unnaturally high streambanks that preclude the formation of natural wetlands and sloughs.

■ **PLANT LIFE AND HABITATS**

Forest Bottomland forest is Seedskadee's crown jewel; mature narrowleaf cottonwoods stand above a deep tangle of coyote and booth's willow, with shrubs such as gooseberry, currant, woods rose, skunkbush, and other woody species.

Wetlands Managed and natural riverine wetlands are here in great abundance as well, including marsh complexes of cattail and bulrush, plus the broad, lush expanses of wet meadow, with such emergent plants as sedges, Baltic rush, alkali bulrush, and creeping foxtail.

Arid lands It wouldn't be Wyoming without sagebrush; the state has more of this semidesert shrub than any other place on earth. At Seedskadee, Great Basin big sage is a dominant species, along with rabbit brush, a close relative. Other shrubs include greasewood and shad scale. June grass and needlegrass are two of several native bunchgrasses here. Wildflowers include evening primrose, larkspur, penstemons, desert paintbrush, and yarrow, among others.

■ ANIMAL LIFE

Birds At least one pair of trumpeter swans nests here each summer, and others may be seen passing through. Nesting raptors are prolific, with no fewer than 20 pairs of red-tailed hawks tending young; visible in early spring, their nests in cottonwoods and mature shrubs are quickly screened by emerging leaves. A pair of prairie falcons nests here, as do golden eagles, northern harriers, and bald eagles, which maintain three active sites.

Mammals Hardly a day goes by without a moose or mule deer wandering in and out of the bottomland thickets; on hot days, in secluded sites, moose enjoy a dip in the river and may be spotted by paddlers. Pronghorn are also common. Wild horses, thought to be descendants of early European stock, inhabit nearby public lands and occasionally move through the refuge. Bobcat, beaver, coyote, porcupine, and river otter are all present as well. Black-tailed and white-tailed jackrabbits are seen bounding around most everywhere.

ACTIVITIES

■ **CAMPING:** Camping is not permitted on the refuge; nearby facilities are located north of the refuge at Weeping Rock, Tailrace, and Slate Creek campgrounds; primitive camping is available to the south on Bureau of Land Management (BLM) lands.

■ **SWIMMING:** Swimming is not permitted.

■ **WILDLIFE OBSERVATION:** The Hay Farm area of the auto tour offers an exceptional experience—golden eagles nesting on a raised platform in an open field; using binoculars or a spotting scope, you can park on the roadside and watch them.

■ **PHOTOGRAPHY:** Great sunrises and sunsets are common at Seedskadee. Portable blinds are allowed in most areas—check with refuge staff in advance. There are also tremendous opportunities for photographing moose along the river.

■ **HIKES AND WALKS:** Two new trails should be complete by the summer of 2000, including a boardwalk crossing the river to an island in the Dodge Bottoms area. Horseshoe Bend is a large cliff with exceptional views of the area.

■ **SEASONAL EVENTS:** Take a Kid Fishing Day is held in late spring.

■ **PUBLICATIONS:** Refuge brochure; historic sites interpretive brochure with map of refuge and adjacent lands.

Appendix

NONVISITABLE NATIONAL WILDLIFE REFUGES

Below is a list of other national wildlife refuges in the Rocky Mountain states. These refuges are not open to the public.

Bamforth NWR
c/o Arapaho NWR
P.O. Box 457
Walden, CO 80480
970/723-8202

Lamesteer NWR
c/o Medicine Lake NWR
223 North Shore Rd.
Medicine Lake, MT 59247-9600
406/789-2305

Mortenson Lake NWR
c/o Arapaho NWR
P.O. Box 457
Walden, CO 80480
970/723-8202

Cokeville Meadows NWR
c/o Seedskadee NWR
P.O. Box 700
Green River, WY 82935-0700
307/875-2187

FEDERAL RECREATION FEES

Some—but not all—NWRs and other federal outdoor recreation areas require payment of entrance or use fees (the latter for facilities such as boat ramps). There are several congressionally authorized entrance fee passes:

■ ANNUAL PASSES

Golden Eagle Passport Valid for most national parks, monuments, historic sites, recreation areas, and national wildlife refuges. Admits the passport signee and any accompanying passengers in a private vehicle. Good for 12 months. Purchase at any federal area where an entrance fee is charged. The 1999 fee for this pass was $50.00

Federal Duck Stamp Authorized in 1934 as a federal permit to hunt waterfowl and as a source of revenue to purchase wetlands, the Duck Stamp now also serves as an annual entrance pass to NWRs. Admits holder and accompanying passengers in a private vehicle. Good from July 1 for one year. Valid for *entrance* fees only. Purchase at post offices and many NWRs or from Federal Duck Stamp Office, 800/782-6724, or at Wal-Mart, Kmart, or other sporting good stores.

■ LIFETIME PASSES

Golden Access Passport Lifetime entrance pass—for persons who are blind or permanently disabled—to most national parks and NWRs. Admits signee and any accompanying passengers in a private vehicle. Provides 50 percent discount on federal use fees charged for facilities and services such as camping or boating. Must be obtained in person at a federal recreation area charging a fee. Obtain by showing proof of medically determined permanent disability or eligibility for receiving benefits under federal law.

Golden Age Passport Lifetime entrance pass—for persons 62 years of age or older—to national parks and NWRs. Admits signee and any accompanying passengers in a private vehicle. Provides 50 percent discount on federal use fees charged for facilities and services such as camping or boating. Must be obtained in person at a federal recreation area charging a fee. One-time $10.00 processing charge. Available only to U.S. citizens or permanent residents.

For more information, contact your local federal recreation area for a copy of the *Federal Recreation Passport Program* brochure.

VOLUNTEER ACTIVITIES

Each year, 30,000 Americans volunteer their time and talents to help the U.S. Fish & Wildlife Service conserve the nation's precious wildlife and their habitats. Volunteers conduct Fish & Wildlife population surveys, lead public tours and other recreational programs, protect endangered species, restore habitat, and run environmental education programs.

The NWR volunteer program is as diverse as the refuges themselves. There is no "typical" Fish & Wildlife Service volunteer. The different ages, backgrounds, and experiences volunteers bring with them is one of the greatest strengths of the program. Refuge managers also work with their neighbors, conservation groups, colleges and universities, and business organizations.

A growing number of people are taking pride in the stewardship of local national wildlife refuges by organizing nonprofit organizations to support individual refuges. These refuge community partner groups, which numbered about 200 in 2000, have been so helpful that the Fish & Wildlife Service, National Audubon Society, National Wildlife Refuge Association, and National Fish & Wildlife Foundation now carry out a national program called the "Refuge System Friends Initiative" to coordinate and strengthen existing partnerships, to jump-start new ones, and to organize other efforts promoting community involvement in activities associated with the National Wildlife Refuge System.

For more information on how to get involved, visit the Fish & Wildlife Service Homepage at http://refuges.fws.gov; or contact one of the Volunteer Coordinator offices listed on the U.S. Fish & Wildlife General Information list of addresses below or the U. S. Fish & Wildlife Service, Division of Refuges, Attn: Volunteer Coordinator, 4401 North Fairfax Drive, Arlington, VA 22203; 703/358-2303.

U.S. FISH & WILDLIFE GENERAL INFORMATION

Below is a list of addresses to contact for more inforamation concerning the National Wildlife Refuge System.

U.S. Fish & Wildlife Service Division of Refuges
4401 North Fairfax Dr., Room 670
Arlington, Virginia 22203
703/358-1744
Web site: fws.refuges.gov

F & W Service Publications:
800/344-WILD

U.S. Fish & Wildlife Service Pacific Region
911 NE 11th Ave.
Eastside Federal Complex
Portland, OR 97232-4181
External Affairs Office: 503/231-6120
Volunteer Coordinator: 503/231-2077
The Pacific Region office oversees the refuges in California, Hawaii, Idaho, Nevada, Oregon, and Washington.

U.S. Fish & Wildlife Service Southwest Region
500 Gold Ave., SW
P.O. Box 1306
Albuquerque, NM 87103
External Affairs Office: 505/248-6285
Volunteer Coordinator: 505/248-6635
The Southwest Region office oversees the refuges in Arizona, New Mexico, Oklahoma, and Texas.

U.S. Fish & Wildlife Service Great Lakes-Big Rivers Region
1 Federal Dr.
Federal Building
Fort Snelling, MN 55111-4056
External Affairs Office: 612/713-5310
Volunteer Coordinator: 612/713-5444
The Great Lakes-Big Rivers Region office oversees the refuges in Iowa, Illinois, Indiana, Michigan, Minnesota, Missouri, Ohio, and Wisconsin.

U.S. Fish & Wildlife Service Southeast Region
1875 Century Center Blvd.
Atlanta, GA 30345
External Affairs Office: 404/679-7288
Volunteer Coordinator: 404/679-7178
The Southeast Region office oversees the refuges in Alabama, Arkansas, Florida, Georgia, Kentucky, Louisiana, Mississippi, North Carolina, South Carolina, Tennessee, and Puerto Rico.

U.S. Fish & Wildlife Service Northeast Region
300 Westgate Center Dr.
Hadley, MA 01035-9589
External Affairs Office: 413/253-8325
Volunteer Coordinator: 413/253-8303
The Northeast Region office oversees the refuges in Connecticut, Delaware, Massachusetts, Maine, New Hampshire, New Jersey, New York, Pennsylvania, Rhode Island, Vermont, Virginia, West Virginia.

U.S. Fish & Wildlife Service Mountain-Prairie Region
P.O. Box 25486
Denver Federal Center
P. O. Box 25486
Denver, CO 80225
External Affairs Office: 303/236-7905
Volunteer Coordinator: 303/236-8145, x 614
The Mountain-Prairie Region office oversees the refuges in Colorado, Kansas, Montana, Nebraska, North Dakota, South Dakota, Utah, and Wyoming.

U.S. Fish & Wildlife Service Alaska Region
1011 East Tudor Rd.
Anchorage, AK 99503
External Affairs Office: 907/786-3309
Volunteer Coordinator: 907/786-3391

NATIONAL AUDUBON SOCIETY
WILDLIFE SANCTUARIES

National Audubon Society's 100 sanctuaries comprise 150,000 acres and include a wide range of habitats. Audubon managers and scientists use the sanctuaries for rigorous field research and for testing wildlife management strategies. The following is a list of 24 sanctuaries open to the public. Sanctuaries open by appointment only are marked with an asterisk.

EDWARD M. BRIGHAM III ALKALI LAKE SANCTUARY*
c/o North Dakota State Office
118 Broadway, Suite 502
Fargo, ND 58102
701/298-3373

FRANCIS BEIDLER FOREST SANCTUARY
336 Sanctuary Rd.
Harleyville, SC 29448
843/462-2160

BORESTONE MOUNTAIN SANCTUARY
P.O. Box 524
118 Union Square
Dover-Foxcroft, ME 04426
207/564-7946

CLYDE E. BUCKLEY SANCTUARY
1305 Germany Rd.
Frankfort, KY 40601
606/873-5711

BUTTERCUP WILDLIFE SANCTUARY*
c/o New York State Office
200 Trillium Lane
Albany, NY 12203
518/869-9731

CONSTITUTION MARSH SANCTUARY
P.O. Box 174
Cold Spring, NY, 10516
914/265-2601

CORKSCREW SWAMP SANCTUARY
375 Sanctuary Rd. West
Naples, FL 34120
941/348-9151

FLORIDA COASTAL ISLANDS SANCTUARY*
410 Ware Blvd., Suite 702
Tampa, FL 33619
813/623-6826

EDWARD L. & CHARLES E. GILLMOR SANCTUARY*
3868 Marsha Dr.
West Valley City, UT 84120
801/966-0464

KISSIMMEE PRAIRIE SANCTUARY*
100 Riverwoods Circle
Lorida, FL 33857
941/467-8497

MAINE COASTAL ISLANDS SANCTUARIES*
Summer (June–Aug.):
12 Audubon Rd.
Bremen, ME 04551
207/529-5828

MILES WILDLIFE SANCTUARY*
99 West Cornwall Rd.
Sharon, CT 06069
860/364-0048

NORTH CAROLINA COASTAL ISLANDS SANCTUARY*
720 Market St.
Wilmington, NC 28401-4647
910/762-9534

NORTHERN CALIFORNIA SANCTUARIES*
c/o California State Office
555 Audubon Place
Sacramento, CA 95825
916/481-5440

PINE ISLAND SANCTUARY*
P.O. Box 174
Poplar Branch, NC 27965
919/453-2838

RAINEY WILDLIFE SANCTUARY*
10149 Richard Rd.
Abbeville, LA 70510-9216
318/898-5969 (Beeper: leave message)

RESEARCH RANCH SANCTUARY*
HC1, Box 44
Elgin, AZ 85611
520/455-5522

RHEINSTROM HILL WILDLIFE SANCTUARY*
P.O. Box 1
Craryville, NY 12521
518/325-5203

THEODORE ROOSEVELT SANCTUARY
134 Cove Rd.
Oyster Bay, NY 11771
516/922-3200

LILLIAN ANNETTE ROWE SANCTUARY
44450 Elm Island Rd.
Gibbon, NE 68840
308/468-5282

SABAL PALM GROVE SANCTUARY
P.O. Box 5052
Brownsville, TX 78523
956/541-8034

SILVER BLUFF SANCTUARY*
4542 Silver Bluff Rd.
Jackson, SC 29831
803/827-0781

STARR RANCH SANCTUARY*
100 Bell Canyon Rd.
Trabuco Canyon, CA 92678
949/858-0309

TEXAS COASTAL ISLANDS SANCTUARIES
c/o Texas State Office
2525 Wallingwood, Suite 301
Austin, TX 78746
512/306-0225

BIBLIOGRAPHY AND RESOURCES

Birds

McEneaney, Terry. *The Birder's Guide to Montana,* Helena, Mont.: Falcon Books, 1993.

McIvor, D.E. *Birding Utah,* Helena, Mont.: Falcon Books, 1998.

Terres, John K. *Audubon Society Encyclopedia of North American Birds,* Avenel, N.J.: Wings Books, 1995.

Botany

Alden, Peter and John Grassy. *National Audubon Society Field Guide to the Rocky Mountain States,* New York: Knopf, 1999.

Benyus, Janine. *A Field Guide to Wildlife Habitats of the Western United States.* New York: Simon and Schuster, 1989.

Coffey, Timothy. *History and Folklore of North American Wildflowers,* New York: Houghton Mifflin, 1993.

Duft, Joseph and Robert Moseley. *Alpine Wildflowers of the Rocky Mountains,* Missoula, Mont.: Mountain Press, 1989.

Ladd, Doug and Frank Oberle. *Tallgrass Prairie Wildflowers,* Helena, Mont.: Falcon Press, 1995.

Mutel, Cornelia Fleischer and John C. Emerick. *From Grassland to Glaciers: A Natural History of Colorado and the Surrounding Region,* Boulder, Colo.: Johnson Books, 1992.

Peterson, Joel G. *Sagebrush: Ecological Implications of Sagebrush Manipulation,* Helena, Mont.: Montana Dept. of Fish, Wildlife & Parks, 1995.

Sutton, Anne and Myron Sutton. *National Audubon Society Field Guides, Eastern Forests,* New York: Knopf, 1985.

Field Guides

Collins, Henry Hill, Jr. *Harper & Row's Complete Field Guide to North American Wildlife, Eastern Region,* New York: Harper & Row, 1981.

Gray, Mary Taylor. *Colorado Wildlife Viewing Guide,* Helena, Mont.: Falcon Books, 1992.

Little, Elbert. *National Audubon Society Field Guide to North American Trees, Western Region,* New York: Knopf, 1996.

Lockman et al. *Wyoming Wildlife Viewing Tour Guide,* Cheyenne: Wyoming Game and Fish Dept., 1995.

Niering, William A. *Audubon Society Field Guide to North American Wildflowers, Eastern Region,* New York: Knopf, 1979.

Peterson, Roger Tory. *A Field Guide to the Birds East of the Rockies,* 4th edition, Boston: Houghton Mifflin, 1980.

Peterson, Roger Tory. *Peterson Field Guides: Western Birds,* Boston: Houghton Mifflin, 1961.

Schmidt, Jeremy and Thomas Schmidt. *The Smithsonian Guides to Natural America: The Northern Rockies,* New York: Random House, 1996.

Sheldon, Ian. *Animal Tracks of the Rockies,* Edmonton: Lone Pine Press, 1997.

Tilden, J. W. and Arthur C. Smith. *Western Butterflies,* Boston: Houghton Mifflin Co., 1986.

Whitaker, John, Jr. *National Audubon Society Field Guide to North American Mammals,* New York: Knopf, 1996.

Mammals

Grassy, John and and Chuck Keane. *National Audubon Society First Field Guide: Mammals,* New York: Scholastic Books, 1998.

Nelson, Richard. *Heart and Blood: Living with Deer in America,* New York: Knopf, 1997.

Petersen, David. *Racks: A Natural History of Antlers and the Animals That Wear Them,* Santa Barbara: Capra Press, 1991.

Rue, Leonard Lee, III. *Sportsman's Guide to Game Animals,* New York: Harper & Row, 1972.

General

Ambrose, Stephen. *Undaunted Courage: Meriwether Lewis, Thomas Jefferson, and the Opening of the American West,* New York: Simon and Schuster, 1996.

Brandon, William. *Indians,* Boston: Houghton Mifflin, 1987.

Duda, Mark Damian. *Watching Wildlife: Tips, Gear and Great Places for Enjoying America's Wild Creatures,* Helena, Mont.: Falcon Press, 1995.

Farb, Peter. *Face of North America: The Natural History of a Continent,* New York: Harper & Row, 1963.

Fletcher, Colin. *River: One Man's Journey Down the Colorado, Source to Sea,* New York: Knopf, 1997.

McKibben, Bill. *The End of Nature,* New York: Doubleday, 1989.

Noss, Reed and Robert L. Peters. *Endangered Ecosystems: A Status Report on America's Vanishing Habitat and Wildlife,* Washington, D.C.: Defenders of Wildlife, 1995.

Stewart, Frank. *A Natural History of Nature Writing,* Washington, D.C.: Island Press, 1995.

Wilson, Edward O. *Consilience: The Unity of Knowledge,* New York: Knopf, 1998.

GLOSSARY

4WD Four-wheel-drive vehicle. *See also* ATV.

Accidental A bird species seen only rarely in a certain region and whose normal territory is elsewhere. *See also* occasional.

Acre-foot The amount of water required to cover one acre one foot deep.

Alkali sink An alkaline habitat at the bottom of a basin where there is moisture under the surface.

Alluvial Clay, sand, silt, pebbles and rocks deposited by running water. River floodplains have alluvial deposits, sometimes called alluvial fans, where a stream exits from mountains onto flatland.

Aquifer Underground layer of porous water-bearing sand, rock, or gravel.

Arthropod Invertebrates, including insects, crustaceans, arachnids, and myriapods, with a semitransparent exoskeleton (hard outer structure) and a segmented body, with jointed appendages in articulated pairs.

ATV All-terrain-vehicle. *See also* 4WD and ORV.

Barrier island Coastal island produced by wave action and made of sand. Over time the island shifts and changes shape. Barrier islands protect the mainland from storms, tides, and winds.

Basking The habit of certain creatures such as turtles, snakes, or alligators to expose themselves to the pleasant warmth of the sun by resting on logs, rocks, or other relatively dry areas.

Biome A major ecological community such as a marsh or a forest.

Blowout A hollow formed by wind erosion in a preexisting sand dune, often due to vegetation loss.

Bog Wet, spongy ground filled with sphagnum moss and having highly acidic water.

Bottomland Low-elevation alluvial area, close by a river. Sometimes also called bottoms.

Brackish Water that is less salty than seawater; often found in salt marshes, mangrove swamps, estuaries, and lagoons.

Breachway A gap in a barrier beach or island, forming a connection between sea and lagoon.

Bushwhack To hike through territory without established trails.

Cambium In woody plants, a sheath of cells between external bark and internal wood that generates parallel rows of cells to make new tissue, either as secondary growth or cork.

Canopy The highest layer of the forest, consisting of the crowns of the trees.

Carnivore An animal that is primarily flesh-eating. *See also* herbivore and omnivore.

Climax In a stable ecological community, the plants and animals that will successfully continue to live there.

Colonial birds Birds that live in relatively stable colonies, used annually for breeding and nesting.

Competition A social behavior that organizes the sharing of resources such as space, food, and breeding partners when resources are in short supply.

Coniferous Trees that are needle-leaved or scale-leaved; mostly evergreen and cone-bearing, such as pines, spruces, and firs. *See also* deciduous.

Cordgrass Grasses found in marshy areas, capable of growing in brackish waters. Varieties include salt-marsh cordgrass, hay, spike grass, and glasswort.

Crust The outer layer of the earth, between 15 to 40 miles thick.

Crustacean A hard-shelled, usually aquatic, arthropod such as a lobster or crab. *See also* arthropod.

DDT An insecticide (C14H9Cl5), toxic to animals and human beings whether ingested or absorbed through skin; particularly devastating to certain bird populations, DDT was generally banned in the United States in 1972.

Deciduous Plants that shed or lose their foliage at the conclusion of the growing season, as in "deciduous trees," such as hardwoods (maple, beech, oak, etc.). *See also* coniferous.

Delmarva The peninsula extending along the eastern end of Chesapeake Bay, separating it from the Atlantic Ocean, including portions of three states: Delaware, Maryland, and Virginia.

Delta A triangular alluvial deposit at a river's mouth or at the mouth of a tidal inlet. *See also* alluvial.

Dominant The species most characteristic of a plant or animal community, usually influencing the types and numbers of other species in the same community.

Ecological niche An organism's function, status, or occupied area in its ecological community.

Ecosystem A mostly self-contained community consisting of an environment and the animals and plants that live there.

Emergent plants Plants adapted to living in shallow water or in saturated soils such as marshes or wetlands.

Endangered species A species determined by the federal government to be in danger of extinction throughout all or a significant portion of its range (Endangered Species Act. 1973). *See also* threatened species.

Endemic species Species that evolved in a certain place and live naturally nowhere else. *See also* indigenous species.

Epiphyte A type of plant (often found in swamps) that lives on a tree instead of on the soil. Epiphytes are not parasitic; they collect their own water and minerals and perform photosynthesis.

Esker An extended gravel ridge left by a river or stream that runs beneath a decaying glacier.

Estuary The lower part of a river where freshwater meets tidal saltwater. Usually characterized by abundant animal and plant life.

Evergreen A tree, shrub, or other plant whose leaves remain green through all seasons.

Exotic A plant or animal not native to the territory. Many exotic plants and animals displace native species.

Extirpation The elimination of a species by unnatural causes, such as overhunting or overfishing.

Fall line A line between the piedmont and the coastal plain below which rivers flow through relatively flat terrain. Large rivers are navigable from the ocean to the fall line.

Fauna Animals, especially those of a certain region or era, generally considered as a group. *See also* flora.

Finger Lakes Eleven long, narrow glacial lakes in central New York State (largest and deepest are Cayuga and Seneca) that were filled with water after the last Ice Age.

Fledge To raise birds until they have their feathers and are able to fly.

Floodplain A low-lying, flat area along a river where flooding is common.

Flora Plants, especially those of a certain region or era, generally considered as a group. *See also* fauna.

Flyway A migratory route, providing food and shelter, followed by large numbers of birds.

Forb Any herb that is not in the grass family; forbs are commonly found in 4WD fields, prairies, or meadows.

Frond A fern leaf, a compound palm leaf, or a leaflike thallus (where leaf and stem are continuous), as with seaweed and lichen.

Glacial outwash Sediment dropped by rivers or streams as they flow away from melting glaciers.

Glacial til An unsorted mix of clay, sand, and rock transported and left by glacial action.

Gneiss A common and rather erosion-resistant metamorphic rock originating from shale, characterized by alternating dark and light bands.

Grassy bald A summit area devoid of trees due to shallow or absent soil overlying bedrock (ledge).

Greentree reservoir An area seasonally flooded by opening dikes. Oaks, hickories, and other water-tolerant trees drop nuts (mast) into the water. Migratory birds and other wildlife feed on the mast during winter.

Habitat The area or environment where a plant or animal, or communities of plants or animals, normally lives, as in an alpine habitat.

Hammock A fertile spot of high ground in a wetland that supports the growth of hardwood trees.

Hardwoods Flowering trees such as oaks, hickories, maples, and others, as opposed to softwoods and coniferous trees such as pines and hemlocks.

Herbivore An animal that feeds on plant life. *See also* carnivore and omnivore.

Heronry Nesting and breeding site for herons.

Herptiles The class of animals including reptiles and amphibians.

Holdfast The attachment, in lieu of roots, that enables seaweed to grip a substrate such as a rock.

Hot spot An opening in the earth's interior from which molten rock erupts, eventually forming a volcano.

Humus Decomposed leaves and other organic material found, for instance, on the forest floor.

Impoundment A man-made body of water controlled by dikes or levees.

Indigenous species Species that arrived unaided by humans but that may also live in other locations.

Inholding Private land surrounded by federal or state lands such as a wildlife refuge.

Intertidal zone The beach or shoreline area located between low and high tide lines.

Introduced species Species brought to a location by humans, intentionally or accidentally; also called nonnative or alien species. *See also* exotic.

Lichen A ground-hugging plant, usually found on rocks, produced by an association between an alga, which manufactures food, and a fungus, which provides support.

Loess Deep, fertile, and loamy soil deposited by wind, the deepest deposits reaching 200 feet.

Magma Underground molten rock.

Management area A section of land within a federal wildlife preserve or forest where specific wildlife management practices are implemented and studied.

Maritime forest Woodland growing near the oceanfront, usually behind dunes, often stunted and composed of pines and oaks.

Marsh A low-elevation transitional area between water (the sea) and land, dominated by grasses in soft, wet soils.

Mast A general word for nuts, acorns, and other food for wildlife produced by trees in the fall.

Meander A winding stream, river, or path.

Mesozoic A geologic era, 230-65 million years ago, during which dinosaurs appeared and became extinct, and birds and flowering plants first appeared.

Midden An accumulation of organic material near a village or dwelling; also called a shell mound.

Migrant An animal that moves from one habitat to another, as opposed to resident species that live permanently in the same habitat.

Mitigation The act of creating or enlarging refuges or awarding them water rights to replace wildlife habitat lost because of the damming or channelization of rivers or the building of roads.

Moist-soil unit A wet area that sprouts annual plants, which attract waterfowl. Naturally produced by river flooding, moist-soil units are artificially created through controlled watering.

Moraine A formation of rock and soil debris transported and dropped by a glacier.

Neotropical New world tropics, generally referring to central and northern South America, as in *neotropical* birds.

Nesting species Birds that take up permanent residence in a habitat.

Occasional A bird species seen only occasionally in a certain region and whose normal territory is elsewhere.

Oceanic trench The place where a sinking tectonic plate bends down, creating a declivity in the ocean floor.

Old field A field that was once cultivated for crops but has been left to grow back into forest.

Old-growth forest A forest characterized by large trees and a stable ecosystem. Old-growth forests are similar to precolonial forests.

Omnivore An animal that feeds on both plant and animal material. *See also* carnivore and herbivore.

ORVs Off-road-vehicles. *See also* 4WD and ATV.

Oxbow A curved section of water (once a bend in a river) that was severed from the river when the river changed course. An oxbow lake is formed by the changing course of a river as it meanders through its floodplain.

Passerine A bird in the *Passeriformes* order, primarily composed of perching birds and songbirds.

Peat An accumulation of sphagnum moss and other organic material in wetland areas, known as peat bogs.

Petroglyph Carving or inscription on a rock.

Photosynthesis The process by which green plants use the energy in sunlight to create carbohydrates from carbon dioxide and water, generally releasing oxygen as a by-product.

Pictograph Pictures painted on rock by indigenous people.

Piedmont Hilly country between mid-Atlantic Coastal Plain and the Appalachian Mountains.

Pine barrens Sandy-soiled areas with scrubby pines and small oaks, typical of coastal mid-Atlantic region. Term most frequently applied to pine forests in southern half of New Jersey.

Pit and mound topography Terrain characteristic of damp hemlock woods where shallow-rooted fallen trees create pits (former locations of trees) and mounds (upended root balls).

Plant community   Plants and animals that interact in a similar environment within a region.

Pleistocene   A geologic era, 1.8 million to 10,000 years ago, known as the great age of glaciers.

Prairie   An expansive, undulating, or flat grassland, usually without trees, generally on the plains of midcontinent North America. In the southeast, "prairie" refers to wet grasslands with standing water much of the year.

Prescribed burn   A fire that is intentionally set to reduce the buildup of dry organic matter in a forest or grassland, to prevent catastrophic fires later on, or to assist plant species whose seeds need intense heat to open.

Proclamation area   An area of open water beside or around a coastal refuge where waterfowl are protected from hunting.

Rain shadow   An area sheltered from heavy rainfall by mountains that, at their higher altitudes, have drawn much of the rain from the atmosphere.

Raptor   A bird of prey with a sharp curved beak and hooked talons. Raptors include hawks, eagles, owls, falcons, and ospreys.

Rhizome   A horizontal plant stem, often thick with reserved food material from which grow shoots above and roots below.

Riparian   The bank and associated plant life zone of any water body, including tidewaters.

Riverine   Living or located on the banks of a river.

Rookery   A nesting place for a colony of birds or other animals (seals, penguins, others).

Salt marsh   An expanse of tall grass, usually cordgrass and sedges, located in sheltered places such as the land side of coastal barrier islands or along river mouths and deltas at the sea.

Salt pan   A shallow pool of saline water formed by tidal action that usually provides abundant food for plovers, sandpipers, and other wading birds.

Scat   Animal fecal droppings.

Scrub   A dry area of sandy or otherwise poor soil that supports species adapted to such conditions, such as sand myrtle and prickly pear cactus, or dwarf forms of other species, such as oaks and palmettos.

Sea stack   A small, steep-sided rock island lying off the coast.

Second growth   Trees in a forest that grow naturally after the original stand is cut or burned. *See also* old-growth forest.

Seeps   Small springs that may dry up periodically.

Shorebird   A bird, such as a plover or sandpiper, frequently found on or near the seashore.

Shrub-steppe   Desertlike lands dominated by sagebrush, tumbleweed, and other dry-weather-adapted plants.

Slough   A backwater or creek in a marshy area; sloughs sometimes dry into deep mud.

Spit   A narrow point of land, often of sand or gravel, extending into the water.

Staging area   A place where birds rest, gather strength, and prepare for the next stage of a journey.

Successional   Referring to a series of different plants that establish themselves by territories, from water's edge to drier ground. Also, the series of differing plants that reestablish themselves over time after a fire or the retreat of a glacier.

Sump   A pit or reservoir used as a drain or receptacle for liquids.

Swale   A low-lying wet area of land.

Swamp   A spongy wetland supporting trees and shrubs (as opposed to a marsh, which is characterized by grasses). Swamps provide habitat for birds, turtles, alligators, and bears and serve as refuges for species extirpated elsewhere. *See also* extirpated.

Tannic acid A brownish acidic substance released by peat and conifers, such as hemlocks and pines.

Test The hard round exoskeleton of a sea urchin.

Threatened species A species of plant or animal in which population numbers are declining but not in immediate danger of extinction. Threatened species are protected under the Endangered Species Act of 1973. *See also* endangered species.

Tuber A short, underground stem with buds from which new shoots grow.

Understory Plants growing under the canopy of a forest. *See also* canopy.

Vascular plant A fern or another seed-bearing plant with a series of channels for conveying nutrients.

Vernal pool Shallow ponds that fill with spring ("vernal") rains or snowmelt and dry up as summer approaches; temporary homes to certain amphibians.

Wader A long-legged bird, such as a crane or stork, usually found feeding in shallow water.

Wetland A low moist area, often marsh or swamp, especially when regarded as the natural habitat of wildlife.

Wilderness Area An area of land (within a national forest, national park, or a national wildlife refuge) protected under the 1964 Federal Wilderness Act. Logging, construction, and use of mechanized vehicles or tools are prohibited here, and habitats are left in their pristine states. Designated Wilderness is the highest form of federal land protection.

Wrack line Plant, animal, and unnatural debris left on the upper beach by a receding tide.

ACKNOWLEDGMENTS

To write a book about the NWR system it is necessary to work closely with a great many refuge professionals—managers, biologists, botanists, information officers—who have made conservation their lives' work. Their knowledge greatly enhanced my own appreciation for what, on any given piece of ground on any given day, is happening in our natural world, both on and off refuges. Their commitment to stewardship impressed me and, in a few instances, even provided a small renewal of hope for the future of wild landscapes and species, which is no mean achievement nowadays. To a person, they answered my questions, corrected my errors, and shared their points of view. Thanks to each and every one of you.

I'm grateful to David Emblidge, the bright light behind this series, for his efforts to keep me organized (a near impossible task) and for his unceasing goodwill, wry humor, and support throughout this project. Alexis Lipsitz and Will Balliett at Balliett & Fitzgerald were helpful and very encouraging. Thanks as well to Amy Hughes, Katherine Santone, and Scott Prentzas for helping me along professionally, and to Erin Turner, Bryan Knaff, and Megan Hiller for friendship and camaraderie.

Closest to home, my wife, Dorothy, acting variously as spouse, editorial consultant, and trained therapist, provided endless support in these and other areas through a most hectic year. Sam, my son, age five, contributed timely interruptions, new drawings for my office walls, and suggestions for future books. I'm lucky to have the both of you.

—John Grassy

ABOUT THE AUTHOR

An editorial consultant for the *Smithsonian Guides to Natural America*, John Grassy also wrote the National Audubon Society's *First Field Guide: Mammals* and its *Regional Guide to the Rocky Mountain States*. He lives with his family in Three Forks, Montana.

PHOTOGRAPHY CREDITS

We would like to thank the U. S. Fish & Wildlife Service for letting us publish photos from their collection, as well as the other contributing photographers for their wonderful imagery. The pages on which the photos appear are listed after each contributor.

Dan Gibson: 5

John & Karen Hollingsworth: 4, 6, 20, 21, 26–27, 28, 33, 36, 39, 40, 42, 49, 54, 58, 63, 70, 75, 78, 82, 84, 99, 101, 101, 102, 107, 110, 115, 118, 120, 124, 126, 129, 132, 138, 144, 145

Gary Kramer: xii, 7, 8, 14, 15, 23, 24, 32, 43, 46, 57, 60, 66, 71, 72, 77, 93, 98, 105, 119, 123, 128, 133, 141, 142

Omni-Photo Communications: 25, 34, 135, 149

U.S. Fish & Wildlife Service: ii–iii, 18–19, 22, 50, 51, 67, 87, 90, 91, 92, 95, 109, 113, 130, 137, 140, 147

NATIONAL AUDUBON SOCIETY
Mission Statement

The mission of National Audubon Society, founded in 1905, is to conserve and restore natural ecosystems, focusing on birds, other wildlife, and their habitats for the benefit of humanity and the earth's biological diversity.

One of the largest, most effective environmental organizations, Audubon has more than 560,000 members, numerous state offices and nature centers, and 500 plus chapters in the United States and Latin America, plus a professional staff of scientists, lobbyists, lawyers, policy analysts, and educators. Through our nationwide sanctuary system we manage 150,000 acres of critical wildlife habitat and unique natural areas for birds, wild animals, and rare plant life.

Our award-winning *Audubon* magazine, published six times a year and sent to all members, carries outstanding articles and color photography on wildlife and nature, and presents in-depth reports on critical environmental issues, as well as conservation news and commentary. We also publish *Field Notes*, a journal reporting on seasonal bird sightings continent-wide, and "Audubon Adventures," a bimonthly children's newsletter reaching 500,000 students. Through our ecology camps and workshops in Maine, Connecticut, and Wyoming, we offer professional development for educators and activists; through Audubon Expedition Institute in Belfast, Maine, we offer unique traveling undergraduate and graduate degree programs in environmental education.

Our acclaimed *World of Audubon* television documentaries on TBS deal with a variety of environmental themes, and our children's series for the Disney Channel, *Audubon's Animal Adventures*, introduces family audiences to endangered wildlife species. Other Audubon film and television projects include conservation-oriented movies, electronic field trips, and educational videos. National Audubon Society also sponsors books and interactive programs on nature, plus travel programs to exotic places like Antarctica, Africa, Australia, Baja California, Galapagos Islands, Indonesia, and Patagonia.

For information about how you can become an Audubon member, subscribe to Audubon Adventures, or learn more about our camps and workshops, please write or call:

National Audubon Society
Membership Dept.
700 Broadway
New York, NY 10003
212/979-3000
http://www.audubon.org/audubon

JOIN THE NATIONAL AUDUBON SOCIETY—RISK FREE!

Please send me my first issue of AUDUBON magazine and enroll me as a temporary member of the National Audubon Society at the $20 introductory rate—$15 off the regular rate. If I wish to continue as a member, I'll pay your bill when it arrives. If not, I'll return it marked "cancel," owe nothing, and keep the first issue free.

____ Payment Enclosed   ____ Bill Me

Name _____

Street _____

City _____

State/zip _____

Please make checks payable to the National Audubon Society. Allow 4–6 weeks for delivery of magazine. $10 of dues is for AUDUBON magazine. Basic membership, dues are $35.

Mail to:

NATIONAL AUDUBON SOCIETY
Membership Data Center
P.O. Box 52529
Boulder, CO 80322-2529